FLOWERS
OF THE
CARIBBEAN

TEXT BY
BRUNO FOGGI

PHOTOGRAPHS BY
ANDREA INNOCENTI

BONECHI

Contents

Publication created and designated by: Casa Editrice Bonechi
Publication Manager: Monica Bonechi
Picture Research: Alberto Andreini
Layout and Make-up: Vanni Berti
Cover: Maria Rosanna Malagrinò
Editing: Patrizia Fabbri and Paula Boomsliter

Text: Bruno Foggi
Translation: Paula Boomsliter

© Copyright by Casa Editrice Bonechi, via Cairoli 18/b Firenze - Italia
Phone +39 055576841 - Fax +39 0555000766
E-mail: bonechi@bonechi.it - Internet: www.bonechi.it

Printed in Italy by
Centro Stampa Editoriale Bonechi - Sesto Fiorentino.

The photographs, by Andrea Innocenti, are property of the Casa Editrice Bonechi Archives.

We wish to extend our special thanks to Dr. Andrew L. Guthrie of the Queen Elisabeth II Botanic Park of the Cayman Islands, GB for the precious information supplied.

Our thanks also to both the Queen Elisabeth II Botanic Park and Fairchild Tropical Garden in Miami, Florida, USA for permission to photograph in the parks.

ISBN 88-476-0626-8

* * *

INTRODUCTION

The Caribbean islands extend in an arc for about 3500 kilometers south from Florida to the northern coast of Venezuela. The climate of the islands is typically tropical, with a wet season from May through November and a dry season from December through April. The mean annual temperature is about 25°C, while annual rainfall exceeds 1000 mm on all the islands but is heaviest on the Jamaican highlands, which receive more than 4000 mm. Precise geographic, climatic, and historical conditions have determined great variety in the typical flora of these islands: there are innumerable wild species throughout the islands, from the coasts to the forests of the interior, which today are in large part natural parks, and many exotic species introduced at different times in history following the European 'discovery' of the archipelago in the late 1400s.

The flora of the Caribbean islands shows strong analogies with that of Central America; so much so that both types are included under the broad definition of 'neotropical' flora. The genesis of the flora specific to the Caribbean region may be said to have occurred in three successive stages. The first coincides with the formation of an independent continental plate midway through the Jurassic period (195-135 million years ago); this first period, the so-called 'Caribbean plate phase', dates the oldest species of Carribean flora, most of which are identifiable with the less evolved types of terrestrial plants, like mosses and ferns. The differentiation of the flowering plants Ravenala and Dracaena may have taken place during this same period. The flora characteristic of this phase shows many analogies with plants of the Canary Islands (Dracaena draco), of Africa, and of Southeast Asia.

In the late Oligocene epoch (37 to 24 million years ago) there began what is generally known as the 'land-bridge phase'. In this time period, the Antilles were for the most part above water and there existed many land bridges linking them to the neighboring terra firma, like the Yucatan peninsula and both North and South America. The differentiation of the species belonging to the genera Bursera, Cassia, Caesalpinia, and Copernicia may be dated to this phase. What is more, in this same period the precursors of today's species of the genus Coccothrinax may have migrated south across a land bridge that linked the south of what is now the United States with the Caribbean islands; these migrations, and subsequent differentiation in loco, ought probably to be presumed to have occurred during periods of dry climatic conditions, given that the adaptations shown by these plants are typically xerophytic. Typically neotropical genera such as Plumeria appear to have been distinguished, in this phase, by a strong tendency toward diversification with consequent formation of a great number of species.

The last and most recent phase is generally known as the 'archipelago phase'. The islands as we know them today were mostly formed by the late Miocene epoch (24 to 5 million years ago), although a few bridges to the continental landmass, like that which through the Cayman Islands linked the Honduras peninsula with Jamaica and Cuba, still persisted. Nevertheless, the tendency toward insularity began to win out, and with time assumed specific connotations such as to differentiate the single islands and the genera present on each. The development of the peculiar floras was the consequence both of isolation and of environmental pressure, a factor which can produce differentiation even on single islands and determine even very strongly accentuated modifications. This phenomenon was particularly significant on the largest of the islands (and therefore, those containing a greater variety of environments). In the case of Cuba, for example, besides the numerous plants endemic to the entire island there also developed a just-as-numerous group of species each of which lived in only one part of the island - and consequently more

important areas as regards preservation of biodiversity: altogether, this archipelago hosts about 13,000 plant species. The profusion of flora on each island depends for the most part on land area and altitude, which are the major factors in determining marked diversification of habitats. It is estimated that the flora of Cuba counts 6500 species, of which 3200 (almost 50%) are found only on Cuba and are therefore defined as endemic; Haiti also boasts a very rich flora counting about 5200 species, of which 1450 (28%) are endemic to the island. On other islands, less pronounced environmental diversification has resulted in a less diversified flora - in the Bermudas, for example, where there are only 166 species with a scarce 10% endemism, or on Antigua, which although it counts 845 species has no endemic species at all.

Unfortunately, however, although on the one hand the peculiar nature of the island environment permits diversification of the endemic species, on than 50% of the species present on Cuba were specific only to this island or to some parts of it. The phenomenon tended to be more accentuated in periods of great climatic changes and tectonic activity; one of these occurred about 1.5 million years ago, between the Pliocene and the Pleistocene epochs, when in the entire northern hemisphere of our planet the climate oscillated continually between warmer and cooler periods.

Today, the Caribbean islands are one of the world's most

the other the isolated conditions make these environments highly sensitive to change. Man has not made a significant contribution to diversification of the species of the Caribbean islands, as instead happened in the Mediterranean area, because it was only after the end of the 15th century that he began to model the environment in earnest. It may, in fact, be said that until the advent of the Europeans, both the Arawaks and the Caribs had lived in perfect harmony with their environment, and that therefore the natural habitat has simply not had time to adapt to the modifications introduced later from outside. It is for exactly this reason that the impact, however late in coming, has been particularly strong, above all if we consider how easily these lands adapted to cultivation. Thus much of the natural island flora, which has had nei-ther the necessary 'strength' to react nor indeed sufficient reaction time (factors, these, which permitted Mediterranean flora, for example, to counter these types of assaults), simply 'suffered' the invasion and became extinct or is now relegated to only the least accessible areas. Many of the Caribbean species are now found in one or only a few stations and are therefore seriously threatened with extinction, while others simply no longer exist in the wild and still persist only thanks to the work of those botanical gardens which have developed specific conservation programs. Many other problems have been caused by the continual importation of exotic species for cultivation for alimentary and ornamental uses. Just think that in the early 1800s almost 95% of Cuba was covered with forests and natural vegetation, while now only 18% of the island's surface still is. Extensive mangrove forests can now be found only on the Cayman Islands, since almost everywhere else they have been destroyed to make space for tourist-oriented developments. In the Bermudas and the Bahamas, natural vegetation is almost nonexistent. The only montane forests still surviving are on Jamaica, Haiti, and, although not as extensively, on some of the Lesser Antilles islands like Dominica, Grenada, and Martinica.

Despite all this, there still do exist examples of typical habitats, each characterized by particular species and types of vegetation:

- sandy and rocky coasts
- mangrove forests
- freshwater wetlands
- forests, scrub woods, savannas, and shrub formations
- anthropized environments.

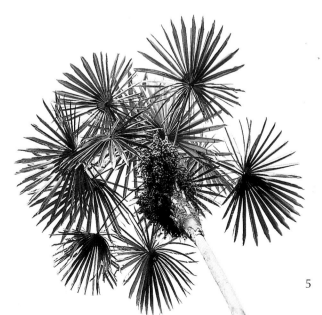

SANDY COASTS AND ROCKY COASTS

Generally speaking, the seacoasts are extremely hostile environments to plant growth. Scarcity of fresh water, sandy substrates that rapidly drain off the water made available by precipitation and thus make it of little utility to the plants, the winds, which tend to cause water to evaporate more quickly, and the saltiness of the air and sometimes also the soil, which reduces the absorption capacity of the root system, all combine to make life very difficult for plants growing along the coasts. For this reason, these plants generally have small, succulent leaves with waxy coatings that reduce water loss through evaporation, root systems that are well-developed near the surface and that do not penetrate deeply into the soil, and, in some cases, even the capacity to expel the salt that accumulates inside the tissues through special surface glands. What is more, the coastal habitat, especially that which develops on sandy substrates, is extremely dynamic: the dunes are produced by the wind moving the sand, and although they are stabilized by the pioneer species, they are also quite apt to suffer the effects of the sea, which sometimes advances inland. The intensity of the influence exerted by each of these factors changes with the distance from the sea, and in general we may say that as we pull back from the coastline all the factors that control the distribution of the coastal plants tend to decrease in intensity. This means that the true coastal plants tend to be concentrated near the sea, while further inland we will find more and more species that are increasingly less tolerant to the effects of the factors listed above.

Typical examples of seacoast environments, where the climate and the morphological characteristics are in the main hostile to plant growth.

The coasts have always been among the preferred areas for the vacation industry, and the constant increase in human settlements along them has caused a marked reduction of the surfaces suitable for the natural formation of coastal habitats; the plants typical of these habitats were the first to suffer from such land use. It takes no great stretch of the imagination to foresee a significant increase in the vacation industry in the years to come, and this will certainly bring more anthropic pressure to bear on these habitats - creating serious risks for the survival of the very environment which draws vacationers from all over the world. It follows, although it should go almost without saying, that the objective of development of the coastal regions for vacation use ought to take forms that are not hostile to preservation of the preexisting natural environments.

One of the most common and certainly most useful coastal species, since it creates shady areas along the otherwise sun-drenched coastlines, is the Coconut Palm (*Cocos nucifera*), but there are also other trees that are almost always present on all the types of coasts, like two members of the genus *Coccoloba* (*C. uvifera* and *C. pubescens*), *Chrysobalanus icaco* or Coconut Plum, and *Argusia gnaphaloides*, a shrub with an unmistakable growth form of densely-woven branches. Among the pioneer species are the herbs *Cakile lanceolata*, *Ipomoea pes-caprae*, *Catharanthus roseus*, and *Cyperus planifolius*, which is common in both sandy and rocky coastal habitats. Along the rocky coasts, which are often derived from ancient coral formations, we also find a number of shrubs that are easily recognizable even though their flowers are tiny: for example, *Suriana maritima*, *Strumpfia maritima*, and *Rachicallis americana*.

Only a few plants succeed in growing on the sand at the very edge of the sea.

COCONUT
Cocos nucifera L. ☐1 ☐2
(Arecaceae)

This tree, which is cultivated throughout the world wherever climatic conditions permit, is easy to recognize thanks to its fruit, the coconut. *C. nucifera* is a palm tree growing to 20 m; the slender trunk may achieve a diameter of 50 cm. The giant leaves, borne at the top of the trunk, are feathery-pinnate and some meters in length. The flowers are grouped by sex in inflorescences up to 1.5 m long. The coconut is a single seed supplied with a great mass of reserve tissue that provides nourishment for the embryo during the first stages of its development.

2

It is not at all unusual for coconuts, which are capable of floating and provided with external tissues that protect the embryo from salinity, to be transported across the oceans to far-off islands and atolls and thus to become the first colonizing plants in many places. Once it has reached land, the coconut puts out a large mass of roots that lend it the stability needed to resist even the hurricanes that often sweep over this area of the world. The origin of the coconut palm is still debated, although it is certain that it was unknown to the first Europeans to reach the Caribbean islands. Today, it is widely cultivated for ornamental, alimentary, and medicinal uses. Coconut oil is used in treating skin ailments, coconut milk possesses diuretic properties, and the pulp is an excellent laxative.

JAMAICAN KINO
Coccoloba uvifera L. ☐3 ☐4
(Polygonaceae)

A tree growing to 15 meters, with a spreading, rounded crown; it sometimes becomes prostrate in places subject to strong winds. The large, leathery, orbiculate leaves are up to 30 cm wide, with markedly protuberant reddish veins. The strongly-scented flowers are very small singly but are grouped in elongated inflorescences of up to 30 cm in length. As one of the first trees to colonize the coasts of the Caribbean islands and southern Florida on both sandy and rocky

1

3

4

5

substrates, *C. uvifera* offers shelter for many birds, lizards, and iguanas. The iguanas, in particular, by eating the fruits favor the dispersal of the seeds. The plant is often used for roadside planting, mainly near the sea, since it is a hardy species that is highly resistant to salt spray and, more generally, to pollution. The fruits are edible and also used to produce an alcoholic beverage similar to wine, which is generally served very cold. The resin that seeps from the bark, which has won for the plant the local name of Jamaican Kino, possesses astringent properties and is used in medicine for treating hemorrhages, diarrhea, and asthma. The other common name of the plant, Sea Grape, derives from the look of its infructescences, which recall bunches of grapes.

Sea Plum
Chrysobalanus icaco L. ⬚5
(Chrysobalanaceae)

This is a small tree, generally 3 to 5 meters tall although 8-meter individuals have been reported, with a rounded, very dense crown. The persistent, leathery leaves are oblanceolate with a retuse apex; they are a shiny dark green in color, lightening somewhat toward the base, and have evident veins that meet at the margins. The small, whitish flowers are grouped in elongated inflorescences borne at the leaf axils. The fruits resemble plums; generally whitish, they tend to reddish in the coastal forms and to dark purple in those growing in the interior. The Sea Plum is spontaneous along the Atlantic coasts of Central and South America, above all on sandy substrates, but is also found in the interior at up to 1000 meters altitude. It is an excellent ornamental for use near the coast, thanks to its high resistence to wind, salt, and parasitic infestation. The fruits are eaten both raw and cooked and would seem to possess curative properties against diarrhea, dysentery, and hemorrhage. In the Spanish-speaking islands, this plant is still called by the name given it by the Arawaks, *hicaco*, a term meaning 'fat pig'.

SEASIDE LAVENDER
Argusia gnaphaloides (L.)
H. Heine [6]
(Boraginaceae)

The single species of the genus
Argusia is distributed throughout the
Caribbean islands, in Florida, and in
western Mexico. It is a small shrub
normally growing no taller than one
meter; near the base, the branches
are woody, leafless, and densely
intertwined, while further up they
are fleshy with many thick, linear,
green-grey leaves. Hidden among
the leaves are the small, whitish
flowers, grouped in the scorpioid
inflorescences typical of the Borage
family. This plant is found along the
coasts of Central America, mainly in
the rocky areas and in particular
those most subject to the action of
the salt-bearing winds. It is currently
not widely used for ornament, but

6

since it is extremely easy to
cultivate and highly resistant to
salinity and arid conditions, we can
expect an increase in such use.
A tea prepared from the leaves is
used in treating gonorrhea, syphilis,
rheumatism, and food poisoning
from fish.

SOUTHERN SEA ROCKET
Cakile lanceolata (Willd.)
O. E. Schulz [7]
(Brassicaceae)

The fifteen species of the genus
Cakile are all strictly associated
with coastal habitats; *C. lanceolata*,
a glaucous green herb growing no
taller than 50 cm, is found in the
Caribbean, in Mexico, and in
southern Florida. The small, whitish
flowers are borne in groups on the
upper portions of the stems. This is
one of the first herbs to colonize the
sandy coasts, and prefers spots
where the waves tend to deposit
accumulations of algae and thus
increase the available nutrients;
moreover, it prefers high
concentrations of both sodium
chloride and the nitrogenous salts.
The plant is rich in vitamin C and is
thus used to combat scurvy; it
would also seem suitable for
treating skin ailments. More
generally, it is often used in the
preparation of a sauce with a
mustard flavor.

7

8

BEACH MORNING GLORY
Ipomoea pes-caprae (L.) R. Br.　8
(Convolvulaceae)

With its light green, leathery leaves, this is perhaps the most beautiful of the various species of the genus *Ipomoea* described in this book. It is a coastal plant found mainly in the sandy areas, where it is one of the early colonizers and an excellent stabilizer of incoherent substrates. The long, creeping branches, which put out roots at the leaf insertion points, may reach 40 meters in length. The flowers of this species emit a pleasant scent that attracts the pollinating insects; they tend to open in the morning – hence the common name of Beach Morning Glory. The leaves are edible, but only in small quantities and after prolonged cooking. The boiled stems would seem to possess anti-tumor properties. In times past, the plant was habitually used by Thai fishermen to treat jellyfish stings, and recent research has demonstrated that it contains antihistaminic substances. In the Bahamas, this species is also known by the common name of Bay Hop.

CAYENNE JASMINE
Catharanthus roseus (L.)
G. Don　9
(Apocynaceae)

It was once thought that *C. roseus* originated in the Caribbean, but we now know that the genus *Catharanthus* is composed of five species, all native to Madagascar, and that *C. roseus* was introduced to Central America only in the 18th century. This is a perennial herb that sometimes creeps for short distances along the ground, with opposite leaves and flowers varying in hue from white through pink to purple. It is widely employed as an ornamental in the coastal regions of tropical countries and often becomes naturalized in disturbed soils. As in the great majority of the Apocynaceae (like *Plumeria*, *Nerium*, etc.), many parts of this plant are poisonous because they contain alkaloids but for the same reason are useful in treatment of a number of serious illnesses. *C. roseus* is in fact the source of ninety alkaloid substances, some of which seem to be efficacious against cancer, Hodgkin's disease, leukemia, and other ailments,

although none has yet obtained official US-FDA approval. All of these agents act by blocking cell division in the metaphase stage of mitosis.

9

STRUMPFIA MARITIMA JACQ. [10]
(NO COMMON ENGLISH NAME)
(Rubiaceae)

S. maritima, the only member of the genus *Strumpfia*, is endemic to the Caribbean islands and southern Florida. The plant is very similar to *Rachicallis americana*, another member of the large Bedstraw family with which it shares the same type of habitat, the rocky coasts. Distinguishing features are its less prostrate growth form, longer and needle-like leaves, and slightly more showy flowers. Although it has not yet captured the attention of the plant nurseries, the species, which is highly resistant to the action of the wind and to salinity, is easy to cultivate and therefore ideal for rock gardens near the sea. Its woody stems are burned as a mosquito repellent.

SEA PURSLANE
Sesuvium portulacastrum (L.) L. [11]
(Aizoaceae)

The branches of this fleshy, prostrate, perennial creeping herb are light green, sometimes flushed red. The leaves are thick, fleshy, elongated, and often aristate. The small, very pretty pink flowers have five petals, each with a short, stiff awn, and are

10   11

arranged along the stem in the leaf axils. This is one of the first plants to colonize the both the rocky and sandy coastal habitats in all tropical areas and is resistant to wind and salinity. It is edible both raw and cooked, but must be soaked repeatedly in order to eliminate the salt accumulated in the tissues before being used as food; on the Asian markets it is sold as a salad green. It is also one of the few plants capable of supplying a constant source of graze for livestock pastured in areas with salty soils. Furthermore, it would seem to be efficacious as a cure for scurvy.

BAY CEDAR
Suriana maritima L. 12 13
(Surianaceae)

S. maritima, distributed throughout all the tropical coastal regions of the world, is the only species of the family Surianaceae to inhabit the Caribbean shores. It is a shrub or small tree growing no taller than 6 meters that is found as far inland as the sea spray reaches, on both

sandy and rocky soils. The sparse, erect branches bear short, linear, succulent leaves; the flowers are small and greenish, and present year-round. The leaves can be used for brewing tisanes useful in the cure of intestinal disturbances; the

gummy exudate of the bark yields a mash that is an excellent medication for toothaches and gum disorders.

13

12

MAHOE
Hibiscus tiliaceus L. [14]
(*Malvaceae*)

H. tiliaceus is often confused with *Thespesia populnea* (see description under *Thespesia grandiflora*). Although like *T. populnea* it is planted along the coasts, all things considered *H. tiliaceus* would seem more suitable for use in the marshy interior habitats. It is variously employed for its medicinal properties: the leaves yield a laxative and emollient tea; the flowers and roots, an infusion used as a remedy for colitis and indigestion, but which is also useful in treating asthma, bronchitis, and liver disorders.

CYPERUS PLANIFOLIUS
L. C. RICH. [15]
(NO COMMON ENGLISH NAME)
(*Cyperaceae*)

This member of the Sedge family is an herb with a cluster of flattened gramineous leaves at the base; hence the species epithet *planifolius*. The leaves are narrow, stiff, and pointed, green when new and reddish-brown when dry. The culm is triangular in section and grows no taller than 50 to 70 cm; at its apex there develop a number of globose inflorescences each composed of many brownish flowers and surrounded by long, leaf-like bracts. *C. planifolius* grows spontaneously in both sandy and rocky coastal habitats in the Caribbean and southern Florida.

* * *

Among the coastal species are also a number of exotic plants that now grow spontaneously in the Caribbean; these include two Malvaceae (*Thespesia populnea* and *Hibiscus tiliaceus*, both native to tropical Africa and often confused), *Casuarina equisetifolia*, a species originating in Australia and first brought in to stabilize the dunes, and *Scaevola frutescens*, which on many of the islands has by now supplanted the spontaneously-growing *S. plumieri*.

RACHICALLIS AMERICANA (JACQ.)
KUNTZE [16]
(NO COMMON ENGLISH NAME)
(*Rubiaceae*)

R. americana, the only species in the genus *Rachicallis*, is found along the rocky coasts of the Caribbean islands and eastern Mexico. It is a prostrate shrub of modest size that is easy to recognize because of its tendency to extend over the rocks and cover them. The small, fleshy leaves are grouped in tufts, which in turn are arranged in verticils. The tiny flowers are borne at the bases of the leaves, on the smaller, terminal branches.

HORSETAIL TREE
Casuarina equisetifolia Forst. & Forst. f. [17]
(*Casuarinaceae*)

This conifer, native to Australia, is planted mostly on the beaches both for ornament and for stabilizing the sandy substrate and preventing erosion. It is fast-growing even on poor soils, since its roots contain colonies of symbiontic bacteria that fix atmospheric nitrogen and so make natural fertilizers available to the tree, which may be quite large (30 to 35 meters in height, with a

15

16

trunk of up to one meter in diameter). The leaves are long jointed needles that recall the stems of the Horsetails (Equisetaceae), hence the species epithet *equisetifolia*.

MANGROVE FORESTS

The mangrove forests or swamps represent a peculiar type of vegetation formation that usually develops along the low coastlines but may also reach inland, as far as ecological conditions permit. The term 'mangrove' actually stands for a group of plants, trees, shrubs, and palms that all exhibit morphological adaptations such as to make them suitable for living in areas with muddy soils that are constantly flooded by water more or less rich in chloride salts, and in which the moving water itself is a constant source of disturbance. These factors obviously set serious limits to plant life, and the plants that live in similar habitats have reacted by evolving various structural modifications and reproductive strategies that permit them to variously deal with each.

In order obviate the effects of the high saline concentrations, the mangroves make use of special filters incorporated in their root systems to limit their intake of sodium chloride, or they eliminate the excess salt in the form of crystals, or they accumulate it in the leaves, which are periodically replaced. Some species use only one of these systems; others exploit more than one simultaneously.

Since the waterlogged mixture of mud and decaying organic matter that forms the substrate in soils that are flooded for most of the year contains very little oxygen, many of the mangroves have evolved a complicated aboveground root system involving respiratory or knee roots (pneumatophores) that emerge from the underground part of the plant or directly from the trunk and contribute to increasing the circulation of air in the roots beneath the mud. The multiple trunks instead contrast the continual stress produced by the tides and flooding, which tends to uproot plants. Many mangroves are viviparous, in the sense that the seeds germinate without ever leaving the parent plant; the young plants are thus helped through the first stages in their growth cycle in protected conditions, and this fact provides a further guarantee for the continuation of the species. In the centuries past, the mangrove forests were seen only as swampy wetland environments infested by mosquitoes, crocodiles, and caimans, to the point that their elimination came to symbolize a sort of sign of the passage of 'progress'. But we have now learned that the functions explicated by the mangrove forests or swamps are instead many. First of all, they are habitats of exceptional naturalistic interest for the great number of species they support, and in absolute terms the habitats containing the greatest biodiversity found anywhere in nature, since here freshwater, saltwater, and terrestrial species coexist with other species capable of exploiting all these types of environments. The naturalist's concern for

The unmistakable mangrove formations, with their closely interwoven roots, branches, and leaves rising from the water.

conservation, however, is not the only argument supporting the need to guarantee protection for this type of habitat: just think that about 75% of the species of commercial value to the fishing industry pass at least a part of their life cycle in these habitats. These forested wetlands are also of fundamental importance for defending the coasts from erosion, since they are capable of absorbing the energy of the tides and the winds: for instance, the only two yachts that survived the fury of Cyclone Tracy that destroyed most of Darwin and the surrounding area (Northern Territory, Australia) in 1974 had sought shelter in a mangrove swamp. This type of vegetation is also essential for the life of the coral barrier reefs, since its intricate root system catches terrigenous sediments before they can reach the reef where they would seriously jeopardize the very existence of the corals, which depend on clear water for their survival. What is more, by holding back the sediments, the mangrove roots act as filters for polluting agents - thus keeping the coastal waters clean.

The species that may be variously considered 'mangrove trees' are about 90 in number worldwide, and belong to 21 different families; more than 30 of these species are found in the Caribbean area. The four most important mangrove species in Caribbean flora are the Common or Red Mangrove (*Rhizophora mangle*), the White Mangrove (*Laguncularia racemosa* Gaertn. f.), the Black Mangrove (*Avicennia germinans*), and *Conocarpus erectus*. The Red Mangrove lives in continually-flooded areas both in the presence of high concentrations of sodium chloride and in almost fresh water, and is therefore found in the salt-water marshes near the coasts and forming a sort of border around coral atolls; the White Mangrove prefers muddy soils and high salinity; *A. germinans*, the Black Mangrove, also tolerates high salt concentrations but prefers drier conditions, and for this reason forms wooded areas behind the 'front lines' manned by the Red Mangroves and in the interior on the atolls - but note that in many areas the Red and Black Mangroves grow side by side. Finally, *Conocarpus erectus* thrives both in subsaline and in purely freshwater environments.

The mangrove forests are always luxuriant, verdant areas with highly characteristic and exceptionally dense vegetation.

RED MANGROVE
Rhizophora mangle L. [18]
(Rhizophoraceae)

The Red Mangrove is unmistakable for its many adventitious roots, which arch out from the trunk into the water, strike at some distance from the parent stem, and send up new trunks, giving rise to an intricate network of branches. While the fruits are still attached to the parent plant, they form a sort of long pod with a rigid pointed tip, the embryonic root; when the pod finally falls, the point is in the correct position to penetrate into the substrate. The propagula can float, and thus at high tide may be transported by the current until they encounter conditions suitable for rooting. The Red Mangrove lives

18

mainly along the coasts but also in the interior, in the lagoons of western Africa, tropical America, Polynesia, and Melanesia.

Mashed, the leaves are used as a remedy for constipation; when brewed as a tea, they are useful in treating intoxications caused by ingestion of poisonous fish. The bark is rich in tannin and therefore a powerful astringent. The dried leaves can substitute tobacco. The Red Mangrove hosts *Crassostrea rhizophorae*, a choice oyster.

BLACK MANGROVE
Avicennia germinans (L.) L. [19]
(Verbenaceae)

The Black Mangrove is a tree growing to 20 meters, with shiny, leathery leaves and small white flowers; its distribution area spans tropical America and western Africa. It thrives in soils with concentrations of sodium chloride similar to, but also much higher than, those tolerated by the Red Mangrove (*Rhizophora mangle*), but only in drier conditions. If we observe the atolls from the air, we will see an unbroken strip of Red Mangrove near the coast while the interior is dominated by the Black Mangroves. One major difference between this and the previously-described species is the organization of their aerial root systems: the aerial roots of *A. germinans* do not grow from the trunk but from the roots; they emerge above the surface in clumps that grow no higher than one meter and are similar in appearance to the bristles of a paintbrush. A tea

19

20

prepared from the bark of this tree is used as a remedy for hemorrhoids, ulcers, and diarrhea, and appears also to possess anti-tumor properties.

BLUTAPARON VERMICULARE (L.) MEARS   20
(NO COMMON ENGLISH NAME)
(Amaranthaceae)

This is a low, prostrate herb with a stem just a little over one meter in length, which, with the succulent leaves, is its major distinguishing characteristic. The tiny white flowers are grouped in small, rounded flowerheads distributed along the upper portion of the caulis. The plant is found where the soil salt concentration is very high (for instance at the edges of lagoons), and often associated with *Salicornia bigelowii* and the Red Mangrove. It grows spontaneously in the Caribbean and in western Africa. Both the stems and the leaves can be eaten cooked as a vegetable.

SEA DISY
Borrichia arborescens DC.   21
(Asteraceae)

The Caribbean area counts three species belonging to the genus *Borrichia*: *B. x cubana* Britton & Wiss., *B. arborescens* DC., and *B. frutescens* DC. The first is found only on Cuba; *B. arborescens* is distributed throughout almost all of the Caribbean islands and along the coasts of Mexico and Florida; *B. frutescens*, instead, is found only on the coasts of the countries facing

on the Gulf of Mexico and in the Bermudas. The last two species mentioned differ in only a few characteristics, and are distinguishable mainly due to the fact that *B. arborescens* tends to become a small shrub with leaves that are glabrous or very lightly covered with silvery down, while *B. frutescens*, which is also silver-haired, has the appearance of an herb; it is mostly perennial but becomes annual in the Bermudas. Both species grow in the same type of habitats: mangrove forests, the edges of tide pools and lagoons where the concentration of sodium chloride is very high, and along the coasts. In Florida, where the two species come into close contact, they tend to hybridize. The leaves can be eaten raw as salad greens.

21

22

24

23

BATIS MARITIMA L. [22]
(NO COMMON ENGLISH NAME)
(Bataceae)

The family Bataceae is composed of four species, two of which are found in the Americas: *Batis americana* L., in northern South America, and *B. maritima* L., in the Caribbean and along the coasts of Central America. The latter species is a small shrub growing no taller than 1.2 meters, with spiny branches and rather fleshy leaves varying in color from light green through yellowish. The flowers are very small and are situated at the base of the leaves on the upper portions of the branches. The plant prefers soils with high salt

concentrations, like those of the lagoon habitats and the mangrove swamps. A tea prepared from the leaves would seem to be efficacious in the cure of venereal diseases, skin ailments, and asthma. The leaves may be eaten raw, boiled, or pureed.

WILD CORAL
Salicornia bigelowii Torr. [23]
(Chenopodiaceae)

An annual herb with an unmistakable look, since its stems, which grow no taller than 50 cm, are formed of a series of jointed sausage-like segments that are green below and reddish above, hence the local common name of Wild Coral. The leaves are no more than small scales at the base of each segment; the flowers are also tiny - so much so as to be visible only under a good microscope - and are located at the base of the segments in the cauline portion of the stem. *S. bigelowii* grows only on hyper-saline soils like those of the lagoons and the mangrove swamps, and on the muddy or slightly sandy soils of the Caribbean islands and Mexico. All parts of this plant are edible either raw or cooked, and are also pickled or preserved in brine.

SEASIDE HELIOTROPE
Heliotropium curassavicum L. [24]
(Boraginaceae)

H. curassavicum, while originating in the tropics of Central America, is

highly resistant to sodium salts in the soil and thanks to this fact pushes northward in its distribution to Arizona and the hyper-saline areas of Death Valley, Nevada; in the Caribbean, it is often found around the mangrove swamps. The Seaside or Alkali Heliotrope has also been naturalized in the hot, dry subtropical climate areas of the Mediterranean, Southeast Asia, and Australia. It is an herb growing to 20 to 60 cm, with simple, linear, alternately arranged bluish-green fleshy leaves. Although the plant is hairless, it is covered with a whitish bloom that rubs off easily. The tiny white flowers are grouped near the top of the plant in the scorpioid inflorescences (coiled cymes) typical of most members of the Borage family. The plant is toxic due to the many alkaloids it contains and is a frequent cause of death among livestock reared in the wild state - except for sheep, in which its only effect is to poison their milk.

LEATHER FERN
Acrostichum aureum L. [25]
(Pteridofitae)

The fronds of this large fern may grow as long as three meters and measure up to 40 cm across. The plant is typical of wet habitats, especially the mangrove swamps of the tropical areas of Central and South America, where it is also cultivated and used as an edging for pools in gardens.

25

FRESHWATER WETLANDS

The freshwater wetland habitats form mainly in flat areas, but because the majority of such areas have been used since time immemorial for agriculture and more recently for vacation establishments, untouched wetlands are now hard to come by: the few remaining freshwater ponds are relicts and have therefore have become the object of conservation efforts. In any case, many of the species that grow spontaneously in these habitats, like those of the genera *Pistia, Nymphaea,* and *Nymphoides,* are so beautiful and of such great ornamental value that they are often cultivated in artificial wet areas created in parks and gardens. From the center of a pond toward its edges, the free-floating plants, the broad-leafed rooted plants, and the band of pond vegetation in close contact with the terrestrials are clearly distinguishable.

The unmistakable green of one of the freshwater wetland areas that are generally found on flat terrain.

WATER LETTUCE
Pistia stratiotes L. [26]
(Araceae)

This is a small herbaceous plant made up of a rosette of leaves that floats on the surface of the water with no contact whatsoever with the substrate. The plant propagates by sending out a great number of stolons, at the end of each of which there forms another rosette. The cuneate leaves are up to 10 cm in length and covered with a dense waterproof down that prevents wetting of the actual leaf surface; the plant thus remains very lightweight and floats easily. *P. stratiotes* will tend to be found at the center of a pond, where the water is deepest.

WHITE WATERLILY
Nymphaea ampla
(Salisb.) DC. [27]
(Nymphaeaceae)

This splendid aquatic herb, easy to recognize at a distance even when not in flower, inhabits the ponds, lakes, and permanent pools of Central and South America and the Caribbean islands. It typically grows in fresh water, but can also live in slightly saline environments. Although the round, fleshy leaves, which may be as wide as 30 cm, float on the surface of the water, the plant is anchored to the bottom by its root system. There is thus a depth beyond which the plants of the genus *Nymphaea* cannot survive - generally about 1.2 meters. The flowers, which can achieve a diameter of 15 cm, are without a doubt the showiest part of this plant, one of the few in its genus with white petals and yellow stamens. The White Waterlily is often cultivated in the ponds and small lakes of tropical gardens.

28

29

WATER SNOWFLAKE
Nymphoides indica
(L.) Kuntze 30
(Menyanthaceae)

The Water Snowflake is an herb
with floating, orbiculate leaves that
grow to 15 cm and are quite similar
to those of *Nymphaea ampla*, with
which it sometimes cohabits. But
although the leaves are similar,
N. ampla and *Ny. indica* belong to
quite different families, the
Nymphaeaceae the first and the
Menyanthaceae the second. Despite
this fact, the only distinguishing
characteristic is the flower: those of
the *Nymphaea* or Water Lilies like
N. ampla are composed of many
linear-lanceolate petals, generally
more than 5 cm in length, enclosing
a great number of stamens; the
flowers of the *Nymphoides* or
Floating Hearts, instead, instead,
have five petals that are hairy on the
margins and no more than 3 cm
long, and five stamens. The flowers

of *Ny. indica* are white. The gardens
are sometimes host to cultivars,
tolerant of the tropical heat, of the
yellow-flowered European species
Ny. peltata (S. G. Gmel.) Kuntze.

* * *

At the edges of the ponds there form
true belts of vegetation in which we
find species with only the roots
immersed in the water, while the
aerial portion always remains above
the surface. These plants mark the
point of passage from aquatic to true
land-based vegetation.

STIGMAPHYLLON
SAGRAEANUM JUSS. 28
(NO COMMON ENGLISH NAME)
(Malpighiaceae)

This is a small shrub growing no
taller than one meter in height,
native to the Caribbean and the
tropical-climate zones of the

Americas, where it is found in both
salt and freshwater wetlands. It is
easy to recognize thanks to its
characteristic flowers: the five bright
yellow petals each have a broad
portion and a filiform portion by
which they are attached to a disk,
again yellow, that bears the lateral
stamens and the central style. The
flowers are arranged in groups of
three to ten at the apices of the
topmost branches.

PRIMROSE WILLOW
Ludwigia octovalvis (Jacq.)
Raven 29
(Onagraceae)

This erect shrub, up to 1.5 meters in
height, is entirely covered by sparse
hairs. The linear-lanceolate leaves are
4 to 10 cm long; the flowers are made
up of four yellow petals alternating
with four leaf-like, linear sepals.
L. octovalvis lives in the swampy
areas of most of the tropical zones.

30▶

BULLRUSH
Typha domingensis Pers. [31]
(Typhaceae)

The species of the genus *Typha* are herbs, growing from 30 cm to 2 meters or more, that inhabit swampy areas and riverbanks throughout the world. The flowers (thousands on each plant!) are grouped together to form elongated sausage-shaped inflorescences (10 to 30 cm) that are brown in color and velvety to the touch. *T. domingensis* grows in the swamps of the Caribbean and Central America, generally forming a sort of edging between the dry land and the flooded areas.

STARLET WISTARIA TREE
Sesbania grandiflora (L.) Poir. [32]
(Fabaceae)

S. grandiflora is a slender, flexuous tree native to tropical Asia. It has become naturalized in Central America and the Caribbean, where it can be found growing along watercourses and in any case in areas that are flooded for at least a part of the year. The leaves are composed of 10 to 30 pairs of leaflets up to 5 cm in length. The flowers are generally creamy yellow but may also be orange tending toward red. The fruit is a legume to 50 cm length.

31

32

FORESTS, SCRUB WOODS, SAVANNAS, AND SHRUB FORMATIONS

During that part of the history of the Caribbean region in which the islands have been in contact with the Europeans, that part of their surface area covered by natural vegetation has progressively contracted. The areas that have most suf-

Different types of forests and woods have always been characteristic elements of the Caribbean landscape.

fered have been the forests, which have been cut for wood for construction and felled and cleared to create cultivable land. Currently, therefore, the forested surface area is extremely limited - only in the most isolated and hard-to-reach areas do tracts of virgin forest still survive. Puerto Rico has only a few remaining areas of virgin forest, while in the Virgin Islands there is none at all left. The impression, since the middle of the last century, has nonetheless been that this state of things is changing: many cultivated areas in the interior were abandoned when it was discovered that tourist-related activities offered more and better work opportunities than did agriculture, and in these cases, the natural vegetation has tended to take back its own and make up for lost time quite rapidly, especially given the almost total absence of factors limiting its development - but the new situation has placed greater pressure on the coastal species, which are now forced to fight for living space.

Despite the changes, certain fundamental types of forests and other natural inland vegetation formations still persist; from the higher to the lower altitudes:

- montane and submontane rainforests
- forests dominated by pines
- mixed forests of evergreens and deciduous species
- deciduous forests and scrub woods
- savannas with scattered palms and trees
- shrub formations with spiny species.

27

MONTANE AND SUBMONTANE RAINFORESTS

This type of forest is extremely rare and can be seen only at very high altitudes, generally above 1000 meters above sea level. The annual precipitation measured in the areas occupied by these forests, which by no coincidence are often shrouded in a thick mantle of clouds and fog, exceeds 2000 mm. The forests are dominated by evergreen tree species (that is, species with persistent leaves) that grow to and higher than 35 meters; the underwood is home to many ferns. The crowns of these trees host a great number of epiphytes (or 'air plants') belonging to the families Bromeliaceae and Orchidaceae. Vegetation formations of this type are impenetrable, due to the many overlaid layers of vegetation of which they are formed, and they are practically inaccessible to the non-specialist visitor.

AECHMEA DICHLAMYDEA BAK. 33
(NO COMMON ENGLISH NAME)
(Bromeliaceae)

The genus name *Aechmea* derives from the Greek *aichme*, which means 'head with lances' and refers to the characteristically acute, rigid spines of the sepals. *A. dichlamydea* grows spontaneously in the shady forests of Trinidad and Tobago and of Venezuela. The leaves are linear-lanceolate, 60 to 100 cm in length, and covered with spiny scales. At their bases, the leaf sheaths widen to form a sort of cup, that fills with water and holds it for a goodly part of the year; particular species of animals and algae live in this lilliputian pond, where they form a tiny ecosystem. The ramified inflorescence may be as long as 50 cm, with whitish branches with reddish streaks. The flowers, from 5 to 20 per branch, are sessile; the petals are yellowish in color.

SQUID ORCHID
Encyclia cochleata
(L.) Lemée 34
(Orchidaceae)

The genus *Encyclia* counts about 150 species of epiphytic and lithophytic orchids distributed through the different countries in the tropical-climate zones of the Americas. Since it is in the area running from Mexico to Guatemala that we find most of the species of this genus, it is logical to suppose that this is the area in which it differentiated and from which it later irradiated toward South America and the Caribbean islands, where about ten species live today. *E. cochleata* is one of the most common orchids of this kind to populate the Caribbean forests, even though it can also be found in southern Florida and in Columbia and Venezuela. It is an erect epiphyte with slightly compressed, pear-shaped pseudobulbs, 25 by 5 cm in size. The elliptical-lanceolate leaves are fleshy. The flowers of the Squid or Cockleshell Orchid the largest of any Caribbean orchid species; the erect inflorescence, as long as 50 cm, bears few, well-spaced flowers. The linear and generally pendent tepals are greenish-yellow in color with an intense purple blush in the lower portion. The labellum, about 3 by 3 cm in size, is deep purple tending toward black but fading at the base to whitish with dark purple striations.

33

FORESTS DOMINATED BY PINES

The pine-dominated Caribbean vegetation formations are found from the mountainous areas to the plains. They often arise on siliceous substrates, generally poor in nutrients; in these conditions, the terrestrial species of the family Orchidaceae, like *Bletia purpurea*, are favored by the presence in their root systems of mycorrhizae, which by increasing the absorbent surface of the roots make these species competitive in the same soils that host the conifers.

BLETIA PURPUREA (LAM.) DC. 35
(NO COMMON ENGLISH NAME)
(Orchidaceae)

A terrestrial orchid with underground pseudobulbs, up to 4 cm in diameter, that are markedly compressed along the dorsiventral axis. The light green linear-lanceolate leaves, 100 by 5 cm, set off the pink, magenta, or whitish flowers with their darker lips. The single flowers may reach 5 cm in length; the elongated inflorescences grouping the flowers may be as long as 1.5 meters. The pine woods on the islands of New Providence and Andros host an orchid identified as *B. verecunda* (Salisbury) R. Br.; it would not, however, seem to merit distinction from *B. purpurea.*

BLUE VINE
Clitoria ternatea L. 36
(Fabaceae)

In all probability, this vine is native to the Old World tropics, but since it has long been cultivated in all the tropical-climate regions of the world and has become naturalized in many areas, it is difficult to pinpoint its origin. In the Caribbean, it is found mainly in the pine forests. The compound leaves are made up of five to nine light green, filmy leaflets. At the base of each leaf, a very short pedicel bears a single flower that generally varies in color from dark to light blue (and to whitish in certain cultivars) and is yellowish or in any event lighter in color toward the center. This is a fast-growing plant that adapts easily to any conditions as long as the mean annual temperature is favorable - and as long as it has a support to climb on.

35

36

MIXED FORESTS OF EVERGREENS AND DECIDUOUS SPECIES

The mixed evergreen and deciduous forests are the vegetation formations that in the Caribbean islands show the greatest differentiation in response to local precipitation, type of substrate, and model of exploitation applied by man.

The mixed forests are generally made up of many strata of vegetation, the highest being the deciduous or evergreen tree species. These formations are distributed from the plains to altitudes of 1000 meters, in areas characterized by a five-to-seven-month dry period; they also succeed in tolerating shorter dry periods, but only on substrates characterized by high runoff.

Shady and luxuriant, the forests of mixed evergreen and deciduous species cover quite extensive areas in the Caribbean.

38

JAMAICAN OAK
Cordia gerascanthus L. — *Catalpa longissima* (Jacq.) Dum.-Cours. 38
(Bignoniaceae)

The genus name *Catalpa* derives from *carawba*, the name given the plants by the native populations of the southern United States. The genus is widely distributed, from North America to China and Tibet and also in some Caribbean islands; the species *C. longissima*, native to Jamaica (where it is known as the Jamaican Oak), Haiti and Martinique, is a tree to 25 meters with fissured-reticulate grey bark. The leathery leaves are ovate-elliptical, occasionally obovate, with entire but slightly undulate margins. The corolla of the tubular flowers is 2 to 3 cm in diameter, and yellowish-white blushed pink with striations that are purple on the outside and yellow within.

SPANISH ELM
Cordia gerascanthus L. 37
(Boraginaceae)

This evergreen or deciduous tree grows to 30 meters, with a trunk 2 to 3 meters in diameter. The bark is smooth and grey or grey-green in young trees, becoming dark green and increasingly cracked and split in older individuals. The leaves are lanceolate; the stamens of the creamy white flowers project beyond the corolla. *C. gerascanthus* is spontaneous in the rainforests of Mexico and the Caribbean.

37

THE GENUS *TABEBUIA*

The genus *Tabebuia* counts about one hundred species of trees distributed in tropical America from Florida to Brazil, and achieves its maximum diversification in the Caribbean, where it is not uncommon for a single island to have many endemic species. The various species of West Indian Boxwood, all trees varying in height from a little over 5 to 30 meters, differ mainly in the form of the leaves and the color and size of the flowers.

BEEF BUSH
Tabebuia bahamensis (Northr.) Britton [39]
(Bignoniaceae)

T. bahamensis (Northr.) Britton, found in the coastal forests of the islands of New Providence and Andros, is endemic to the Bahamas where it is known by the local common name of Beef Bush. This small tree, growing no taller than 4 to 5 meters, has digitate leaves divided into five segments, each 3 to 4 cm in length. The campanulate flowers are pink with darker, more or less evident veinings.

39

41

42

WHITE CEDAR
Tabebuia pallida (Lindl.) Miers. [40]
(Bignoniaceae)

T. pallida grows spontaneously in the low-altitude rainforests of the Caribbean islands. The species epithet and the local common name of White Cedar both refer to the flowers, which are white or very light pink with a

40

dark spot within. The leaves are digitate like those of *T. bahamensis*, but with only three lobes.

YELLOW CEDAR
Tabebuia serratifolia (Vahl) Nichols. [41] [42]
(Bignoniaceae)

T. serratifolia, or Yellow Cedar, grows spontaneously in the Caribbean and the Atlantic regions of Central and South America. Its compound leaves have five leaflets with finely dentate or 'serrated' margins; hence the species epithet. The flowers are bright yellow.

43

44

SPANISH MOSS
Tillandsia usneoides (L.) L. [43]
(Bromeliaceae)

This is an epiphyte herb that grows on almost all the trees in the Caribbean and on power and telephone lines as well. Its roots have lost their absorbent function, which is instead expedited by special hairs that cover the entire surface of the plant; these hairs are so efficient that they succeed in procuring all the needed water and nutritive salts directly from the atmosphere. They also lend the plant its characteristic silvery grey color, which is responsible for the species epithet - since *T. usneoides* greatly resembles some members of the lichen genus *Usnea*. The tiny flowers tend to be nocturnal and to bloom during the warmest months of the year. A tea prepared from this plant would seem to be useful in curing infantile liver disorders, and is also used to lower blood sugar levels. Many native populations of the region used the plant in the preparation of poultices for wounds, since it contains a proteolytic enzyme that contributes to promoting fast healing.

BARBADOS LILY
Hippeastrum puniceum (Lam.) Urban [44]
(Amaryllidaceae)

H. puniceum, which grows spontaneously in the tropical-climate areas of the Americas, is a bulbous herb to 30 to 60 cm, with linear leaves. At maturity it produces a scape which just exceeds the leaves in height and at its apex bears two to four flowers that are red-orange on the outside and cream-colored within. In nature, the plant prefers open areas at altitudes from 500 to 1000 meters, but it is also much cultivated. The bulb contains a toxin that causes vomiting and diarrhea.

WAX MALLOW
Malvaviscus arboreus Cav. var. *mexicanus* Schldl. [45]
(Malvaceae)

Although this shrub strongly resembles a hibiscus, it is nevertheless easy to distinguish thanks to its flowers, the petals of which remain wrapped around the style so that only its terminal portion exits the involucre. The flowers are bright red, although there also exist cultivars with pink blossoms. Unlike the genus *Hibiscus*, which is native to central Asia, the genus *Malvaviscus* originated in the semi-deciduous forests of tropical America. In the Cayman Islands and on Cuba we find a variety with very small flowers: *M. arboreus* var. *cubensis* Schlecht.

45

DECIDUOUS FORESTS AND SCRUB WOODS

These are communities in flux, which in any case have a dense cover in the shrub and low tree strata and in which palms of the genus *Coccothrinax* often abound. They are often classified as *monte seco* or 'dry forest' vegetation formations, and in fact they form in areas with a seven-to-nine month dry season with precipitation not exceeding 1000 mm annually. In some cases they may become palm-studded savannas, another formation distinguished by the presence of many species of *Coccothrinax*.

Low, dense brush cover is typical of the deciduous forests and scrub woods.

THE PALMS OF THE GENUS *COCCOTHRINAX*

The genus *Coccothrinax* counts about thirty species of palms distributed throughout the Caribbean area. They are all trees with a well-defined trunk, only rarely branched, that grows to 12 meters height; it is covered with fibers derived from the old leaf sheaths and sometimes possesses long, strong spines. The leaves are palmate, with a petiole that is grooved on the upper surface and as long as one meter; the leaf blade is composed of acuminate segments that are generally silvery in color. The leaves do not fall but rather die, wither and rot on the tree. The flowers are grouped in long, pendulous, branched inflorescences.

GUANO
Coccothrinax argentea (Lodd. ex Schult.) Sarg. ex Becc. **46**
(Arecaceae)

C. argentea grows to 12 meters; its trunk, which can achieve a diameter of 10 cm, is covered with cobwebby fibers. The leaves are 60 to 80 cm across, with a typically silvery underside that reflects the sunlight when the leaves are stirred by the wind, and are not resistant to tearing as are those of *C. proctorii*.
C. argentea is one of the most common palms in the degraded coastal woodlands on the Caribbean islands. The dark brown to blackish fruits are edible; the tree is also a prized ornamental species, thanks to the color of its leaves. On Puerto Rico and in the Virgin Islands we instead find *C. alta* (Cook) Becc., which is very similar to *C. argentea* except for the trunk fibers, which are straw-colored.

46

its fruit, which is white but becomes dark red when ripe.

SILVER PALM
Coccothrinax miraguama (Humb., Bonpl. & Klotzl.) Becc. ssp. *miraguama* 49
(Arecaceae)

C. miraguama is also native to Cuba; it differs from *C. crinita* in having less rigid but much longer leaf segments - up to 65 cm. This species is divided into two subspecies, *C. miraguama* ssp. *miraguama* and *C. miraguama* ssp. *roseocarpa*; the fruit of the first is reddish, while that of the second is rosy in color.

47

SILVER PALM
Coccothrinax proctorii Read 47
(Arecaceae)

This endangered species now grows spontaneously only on Grand Cayman Island in the Woodland Preserve managed by the Queen Elizabeth II Botanic Park. It is very similar to *C. argentea*, differing only in its smaller trunk and the laminar, not cobwebby, texture of its trunk fibers - and in its leaves, which are very strong thanks to the greater quantity of fiber incorporated in the blades. Ironically, this very feature, which makes the species more suitable *C. argentea* or even the Jamaican *C. jamaicensis* Read for fabricating utensils and therefore more valuable, has also much contributed to placing it in serious danger of extinction.

OLD MAN PALM
Coccothrinax crinita Becc. 48
(Arecaceae)

C. crinita Becc., or Old Man Palm, is widespread on Cuba. It differs from *C. argentea* in having a more massive trunk covered with long and fine but not cobwebby fibers, and in

48

49

THE GENUS *PLUMERIA*

The genus *Plumeria* is native to the tropical-climate zones of the Americas, where we find no less than 45 species known by many different names, among which Frangipani, Pagoda Tree, and West Indian Jasmine. The members of the genus are trees with spreading but not dense crowns and fleshy branches, the peculiar appearance of which is due to their being dichotomously ramified from the base to the outermost twigs. Each branch bears clusters of leaves only at the extremities; for this reason the crown cannot provide much shade. The leaves of all but one of the species are caducous, even though they tend to persist on the plant for very long periods (the exception is *P. obtusa*, the only evergreen of the genus); they all also contain a white juice (latex) that while highly toxic can be used to cleanse open wounds. The various parts of the plants are said to possess many therapeutic virtues, but must be administered with care due to their high toxicity.
In pharmacology, they are used to produce cardiac stimulants, anaesthetics, and bacteriostatic preparations and are also employed in treatment of poliomyelitis.

51

WEST INDIAN JASMINE
Plumeria alba L. 50 51
(Apocynaceae)

P. alba grows to 8 meters in the forests near the coasts in the central Caribbean. Its leaves are lanceolate, 15 to 30 cm long and 2 to 3 cm wide in the wild forms, wider in the

cultivated varieties. The highly fragrant white flowers are borne on the outermost twigs of the crown. This species is very similar to *P. rubra*, which, although it is native to Mexico, is cultivated nearly everywhere in tropical-climate areas. The flowers of the wild forms of *P. rubra* are red; the flowers of the

50

52

both provide reliable clues for identification of the different forms: the flowers of *P. rubra* f. *acutifolia* (Poir.) Woodson have a white corolla and the leaves acute tips; the flowers of *P. rubra* f. *lutea* (Ruiz & Pav.) Woodson have a yellow corolla blushed with red; those of *P. rubra* f. *tricolor* (Ruiz & Pav.) Woodson, a pink-edged white corolla and a yellow throat.

FRANGIPANI
Plumeria obtusa L. 53
(Apocynaceae)

This is the only species of this genus to have truly persistent leaves. It is a tree to 8 meters, with glabrous, dully glossy obovate leaves to 20 cm, obtuse at the apex and having a petiole up to 5 cm in length. The yellow-throated white flowers have a tube about 2.5 cm in length and five lobes each 2 to 3 cm long, and are grouped by fours to sevens in inflorescences borne on peduncles 4 to 10 cm in length. This highly variable species is found in the forests of the majority of the Caribbean islands, and is native to the Bahamas and the Greater Antilles. On Cuba, Haiti, and the Yucatan peninsula we find a variety with leaves that are pubescent on the underside: *P. obtusa* var. *sericifolia* (C. H. Wright) Woodson. On Puerto Rico, a *P. portoricensis* Urban is reported; however, it would not seem to differ in any true sense from the previously-mentioned variety.

53

cultivated forms are instead white, and this fact makes these plants difficult to distinguish from the true *P. alba*.

RED JASMINE
Plumeria rubra L. 52
(Apocynaceae)

The Red Jasmine, native to Mexico and the region around Panama, is a

tree to 7 meters and with very heavy branches. The obovate and broadly elliptical leaves, which may be as long as 40 cm, are light green in color with evident venation and a connecting vein along the edges. The fragrant flowers are pink with a throat varying in color from yellow through gold and bronze to pink, or a combination of these colors. Like the flower color, the appearance of the leaves is highly variable - and

55

GEIGER TREE
Cordia sebestena L. 54
(Boraginaceae)

Although the genus *Cordia*, which counts 250 species, is distributed throughout the tropical-climate areas of the world, the majority of its members live in the tropical regions of the Americas. *C. sebestena* is native to the scrub woods of the Caribbean islands; in the early 1900s it was introduced to the tropical Key West off southern Florida by the navigator John Geiger. The tree is small, growing to no more than 8 meters, with a slender, graceful trunk and broad leaves that are very rough to the touch. The flowers, up to 5 cm in diameter, are orange or scarlet red and strongly resemble those of the cultivated geraniums of the genus *Pelargonium*. *C. rickseckeri* Mill. (Puerto Rico and the Virgin Islands) is a related species, quite similar to *C. sebestena*; *C. dillenii* Spring., reported as a species in the Bahamas, should instead be considered a synonym for *C. sebestena*. Because of its pretty flowers, which bloom for most of the year, this plant is widely cultivated as an ornamental.

JUMBY BEAD BUSH
Erythrina corallodendron L. 55
(Fabaceae)

The genus *Erythrina* is quite complex, counting more than 150 species with distribution areas covering practically all the tropical-climate areas of the world, since many different species have been introduced for ornamental purposes. *E. corallodendron* is native to the Caribbean region, where it grows spontaneously in the coastal forests. It is a small deciduous tree to 3 meters, with pinnate leaves with three leaflets resembling the leaves of ivy. The species is easy to recognize thanks to the recurved spines on the stems and the petioles. The coral-red flowers, which have earned for this plant its species and common name of *corallodendron* (Coral Tree), are grouped in conical terminal inflorescences as long as 30 cm. Although folk tradition attributes it near-miraculous powers in curing certain illnesses (like asthma), the plant also contains many dangerous substances including a hallucinogenic alkaloid and another with effects similar to those of curare.

PEREGRINA
Jatropha integerrima Jacq. 56
(Euphorbiaceae)

Many members of the shrub genus *Jatropha*, native to Central and South America, are of high ornamental value; *J. integerrima* is spontaneous on Cuba, but may also be found in gardens in various tropical countries. It is a medium-sized shrub with entire, shiny, light green leaves with a lanceolate blade and an acute apex and sometimes with two basal lobes. The flowers, grouped in terminal inflorescences, each have five lanceolate petals that contrast attractively with the brilliant yellow anthers. Among the species of *Jatropha* most worthy of note are *J. multifida* L. (known by the common name of Coral Plant due to the flowers, which recall bits of coral), distributed in the Atlantic tropical-climate regions, with deeply-cut, fan-like palmate leaves, and *J. podagrica* Hook., native to Central America, with its distinctive barrel-like stem.

56

57

58

PETITIA DOMINGENSIS JACQ. [57]
(NO COMMON ENGLISH NAME)
(Verbenaceae)

A small tree to no more than
13 meters, the bark of which peels off
in the form of large scales. The ovate-
lanceolate, acuminate leaves are up
to 24 cm in length and borne on long
petioles; the underside of the blade is
yellowish in color and puberulent,
with many small glands. The small
flowers, borne in clusters, are also
yellowish. The plant grows
spontaneously, above all in degraded
woodland areas, but is also cultivated.

* * *

The most markedly thermophytic and
thermoxerophytic species are
naturally found in the driest areas,
above all along the coasts on
calcareous substrates derived from
coral formations.

CLUSIA FLAVA JACQ. [58]
(NO COMMON ENGLISH NAME)
(Clusiaceae)

C. flava is a small tree that grows on
rocks or on other plants in the
woodlands near the coast, on dry
calcareous substrates but also in
damp areas. The thick, leathery leaves
are 6 to 15 cm long and 3 to 10 cm
wide; the flowers are yellow or
creamy white, sometimes streaked
with pink, and have four petals 2 to
2.5 cm in length. The juice of this
plant repels water and is used for
waterproofing boats.

59

SLIPPER SPURGE
Pedilanthus
tithymaloides (L.) Poit. [59]
(Euphorbiaceae)

P. tithymaloides is the best-known
species in the genus. It is a succulent
shrub native to tropical America,
growing to 60 cm, with branches
that zigzag somewhat in the distal
portion. The leaves, distributed along
the entire length of the stem, are
broadly elliptical, thick, and waxy, in
variegated tones of light and dark
green, with a short and slightly
winged petiole. The small, bright red
flowers are arranged in pairs, which
in turn are grouped at the apices of
the branches. This plant, like the
majority of the members of the
family Euphorbiaceae, produces a
milky exudate; it can severely irritate
the skin on contact and if ingested
can be fatal.

60

combating menstrual cramps, diarrhea, hemorrhoids, and bronchitis. The seeds contain large quantities of caffeine, which are extracted for industrial uses.

SAGE HOLLY
Turnera diffusa Willd. in Schult. [61]
(Turneraceae)

This species differs from *T. ulmifolia* in having much smaller leaves (rarely longer than 3 cm) with yellow glands on the underside of the blade.

SAILOR'S BROOM
Melochia tomentosa L. [62]
(Sterculiaceae)

This shrub, at most 2 meters in height, is found only in the Caribbean islands and, here, mainly in the disturbed woodlands, from which it spreads along the roadsides and into other disturbed habitats. The whole plant is covered with a dense velvety tomentum. The alternate, ovate-lanceolate leaves have short-toothed margins and prominent nervations; at the base are narrow, linear, bristle-like stipules. The purplish-red flowers, arranged in groups, appear between December and April.

61

62

WEST INDIAN HOLLY
Turnera ulmifolia L. [60]
(Turneraceae)

In southern Florida and the Bermudas, *T. ulmifolia* inhabits the degraded coastal forests; on Cuba, instead, the species tends to prefer the shrub-studded savannas on serpentine soils. It is a small shrub no taller than 3 meters, with stems that are herbaceous when young. The alternate, lanceolate leaves are 4 to 15 cm long and, as the species epithet suggests, similar in appearance to those of the elms. The flowers are light yellow and up to 5 cm in diameter, with five petals. The West Indian Holly is grown as an ornamental in many tropical countries. The leaves contain cyanogenetic compounds useful in defense against insects and also for preparing infusions used for

63

64

YELLOW ELDER
Tecoma stans (L.) Juss. ex
Humb., Bonpl. & Klotz [63]
(Bignoniaceae)

This shrub, native to Central and
South America, where it grows to
8 meters, has compound leaves as
long as 10 cm, with 5 to 13 leaflets.
The yellow, campanulate flowers are
borne in terminal inflorescences and
are present year-round. The Yellow
Elder is common along the roadsides
and in abandoned areas and is the
official flower of both the U.S. Virgin
Islands and the Bahamas.

PORTIA TREE
Thespesia grandiflora DC. [64]
(Malvaceae)

The genus *Thespesia*, of the Malva
family (like the hibiscus, cotton, etc.),
counts twenty species distributed in
the majority of the tropical-climate
areas. In the Caribbean, we find two
species, *T. populnea* and
T. grandiflora. The first is far and away
the most common, above all along
the coasts, while *T. grandiflora* grows
spontaneously only on Puerto Rico -
although it is cultivated throughout
Central America. These two species,
which are very similar as to both
habit and leaf form, are cleanly
differentiated by their flower color:

T. grandiflora has orangey-red flowers
with blackish spots along the central
veining of the petals, while the flowers
of *T. populnea* are yellow with brown
spots in the basal portion of the petals.

CUCUMAN
Guettarda krugii Urban [65]
(Rubiaceae)

A small tree with opposite, persistent
leaves on its few flexuous branches.

The leaves are elliptical to rounded
or ovate, and densely hairy on both
sides of the blade. The fragrant
flowers are brown and covered by a
dense white down; the corolla is
formed of a tube to 2.5 cm opening
into 5 to 8 lobes, each about 1.5 cm
long. *G. krugii* Urban grows in the
woods on calcareous substrates on
Puerto Rico - where it is called
cucuman - and in the Bahamas.

65

SAVANNAS WITH SCATTERED PALMS AND TREES

The savannas are grassland formations (dominated by gramineous herbs) that generally develop in flat areas on arid substrates of both calcareous and siliceous origin but also in areas that flood during the rainy season. The growth period of the plants making up these formations coincides with the dry season, which in the case of the Caribbean can last from 6 to 8 months. Like others around the world, the Caribbean savannas are characterized by a community of low herbs, while the shrub or small tree component, which is generally well-represented, is made up above all of palms or scattered shrubs and small trees distributed in the concentrations typical of the phase of establishment (or reestablishment) of xerophilous deciduous scrub woodlands or forests. The origin of the savannas is a topic of scientific debate; two main theories are that 1) the savannas have always existed and the activity of man has contributed only to extending them, and 2) that these formations are derived exclusively from the destruction of preexisting forest vegetation by natural phenomena or cutting, firing, and grazing. The latter activity is generally considered to have the effect of maintaining the savanna formation stable over time.

CUBAN ROYAL PALM
Roystonea regia (Humb., Bonpl. & Klotzl.) Cook [66]
(Arecaceae)

The Cuban Royal Palm is large - easily over 25 meters height - and is recognizable without difficulty thanks to its trunk, which is wide at the base and progressively thinner above, although it sometimes thickens again toward the top especially in the taller individuals. The lower portion of the trunk is light grey marked by horizontal striations that are lighter in color than the rest of the bark. Above the striated portion, the trunk becomes smooth and light green in color, due to the intertwined leaf sheaths with which it is covered. Above the green portion we begin to see the leaf petioles, which support pinnate leaves that in the tallest individuals may be as long as 6 meters. Thanks to its size and its general habit, *R. regia* is the ideal palm for roadside plantings.

THE GENUS *COPERNICIA*

The genus *Copernicia* is made up of about 70 species distributed on the western islands of the Caribbean archipelago. The plants are palms with a shrub or low tree habit. The segments of the palmate leaves, borne on spiny-margined petioles, are fused together to differing degrees. The inflorescences are elongated and densely ramified, being formed, in practice, of the union of various smaller, superposed inflorescences, the branches of which are sheathed by more or less well-developed spathes.

▼ 67

▼ 68

69

PETTICOAT PALM
Copernicia macroglossa Wendl. & Becc. [67]
(Arecaceae)

The Petticoat Palm owes its common name to the fact that its large, palmate leaves stand erect while they live but when dead remain attached to the trunk and fold downward around it to form a sort of 'skirt' reaching to the ground. This is a sturdy palm that does not grow to great heights. The leaves are divided into about 60 segments, each 100 to 120 cm long; the petiole is short and thick with curved one-centimeter spines and with short-toothed margins. The inflorescence is hairy, especially during the early phases of its growth. *C. macroglossa* Wendl. & Becc. is found on Cuba and Jamaica.

YAREY
Copernicia baileyana Leon [68]
(Arecaceae)

This species of *Copernicia* differs from the others illustrated here in having a column-like trunk and an apical tuft of foliage in which even the dead leaves persist for long periods.

GUANO BLANCO
Copernicia glabrescens
Wendl. & Becc. [69]
(Arecaceae)

The leaves are made up of fifty to
sixty segments, each 50 to 80 cm
long and fused the one to the next
for about half their length. The
petiole is as long as the leaf blade
and is supplied with 6 to 8 mm
spines with a wide base and a
blackish point. The inflorescences
are glabrous all over; it is this
characteristic that distinguishes this
species from the other members of
the genus *Copernicia*.

BRUNFELSIA NITIDA BENTH. [70]
(NO COMMON ENGLISH NAME)
(Solanaceae)

This member of the genus
Brunfelsia grows only in the tree-
studded savannas on the
serpentine soils of Cuba. *B. nitida*
Benth. is a small shrub to 2 meters
height, with ovate-elliptical leaves
which, differently from the other
species mentioned, are light ashy-
green in color. The solitary flowers
are light yellow, with a slender
tube and spreading petals that are
deeply cut into two lobes at the
apex.

BRUNFELSIA JAMAICENSIS
GRISEB. [71]
(NO COMMON ENGLISH NAME)
(Solanaceae)

B. jamaicensis Griseb. is
distributed in the tree-studded
savannas on the majority of the
Caribbean islands, but it was first
discovered on Jamaica; hence the
species epithet. This plant is very
similar to *B. plicata*, also
discovered on Jamaica, and the
two can be confidently treated as
a single species. *B. jamaicensis* is
a low shrub to 1.5 meters with
branches that are minutely
pubescent especially when young.
The oblong-lanceolate obtuse
leaves are first membranous, then
leathery, with prominent veinings.
The flowers are white when they
first open and later become
yellowish in color; they may be as
wide across as 6 cm; pedicels at
most one cm in length support the
slender tube.

70

71

SHRUB FORMATIONS WITH SPINY SPECIES

In the semi-desert areas along the coasts - where the dry season lasts for seven to eleven months and annual precipitation is about 300 to 800 mm - and above all on calcareous soils, there develops a pre-desert ecosystem with vegetation formations characterized by species with marked adaptations such as to permit them to tolerate long periods of drought. The type of habitat is dominated by species *ad habitum cactaceum* (members of the family Cactaceae), large rosette-forming herbs with prickly leaves belonging to the genus *Agave*, and many different trees and shrubs, often spiny, belonging to the families Fabaceae and Caesalpiniaceae.

The enchanting panorama of shrubland dominated by spiny species against the blue background of sea and sky.

CENTURY PLANT
Agave missionum Trel. [72]
(Agavaceae)

The genus *Agave* is composed of more than 300 species, all spontaneous in the arid regions of Central America and the Caribbean and all very similar and therefore difficult to individuate. *A. missionum* and *A. sobolifera* are two of the largest species found in the Caribbean region. The first, spontaneous on Puerto Rico and in the Virgin Islands, is a perennial herb with very large leaves (up to 1.5 meters length and 30 cm width) forming a basal rosette; the apex of the leaf is transformed into a strong spine. At maturity, a scape develops at the center of the rosette and grows to 7 to 8 meters, bearing at its top a heavy greenish-yellow inflorescence. But flowering occurs only when a sufficient quantity of nutrients has accumulated in the rosette - and this process requires many years: from 10 to 80. The rosette dies after flowering (usually March-April), when the nutrients are exhausted, although it generally then produces some basal side shoots. This agave, also called Maguey, grows spontaneously in the degraded woodlands near the coasts in the Caribbean region. The leaves of the agaves are often used as a source of textile fibers like sisal, which takes its name from another species of the same genus, *A. sisalana* Perring. A sweet juice extracted from the young flower spikes of *A. missionum* is fermented to produce a beverage called pulque that is the source of mescal. The leaves, instead, yield a juice possessing astringent properties that is used in treatment of dysentery and certain skin diseases. This plant is pollinated by birds and bats.

CENTURY PLANT
Agave sobolifera Salm.-Dyck [73]
(Agavaceae)

Quite similar to the previously-mentioned species, but having a decidedly fuller inflorescence and basal leaves up to 2 meters in length, which therefore form a larger rosette. *A. sobolifera* Salm.-Dyck is spontaneous on the Caymans and other Caribbean islands, on calcareous substrates of coral origin.

72

73

BAY-LEAVED CAPER
Capparis flexuosa (L.) L. 74
(Capparaceae)

C. flexuosa is a straggling shrub whose branches tend to elongate and simulate the behavior of a vine. The persistent leaves are elliptical, often with a rounded or retuse apex, and leathery in consistency. The richly fragrant flowers are made up of four yellowish-white sepals, four white or very light pink petals, and a great many pure white stamens. The fruits are a medley of color: green on the outside and brilliant red inside, with white seeds. This member of the Caper family is found in the low-altitude forests of Central America, the Caribbean, and South America.

74

75

76

77

SPANISH BAYONET
Yucca aloifolia L. 75
(Aloeaceae)

The genus *Yucca* originated in Central America and the Caribbean; *Y. aloifolia* is native to the rocky coastal habitats in these areas, but is cultivated in the gardens of Central America and indeed of arid tropical regions worldwide. Its trunk is only rarely branched and is more or less deeply embedded in the soil; it grows to 6 meters and terminates in a rosette of rigid, linear, prickly leaves that are green in color or, in the cultivated varieties, green with yellowish striations. The yellowish-white flowers are grouped in an apical inflorescence as long as half a meter. This species is often planted for ornamental reasons, and forms an impenetrable barrier that requires little care. The fibrous leaves are used in basket-weaving; the edible flowers often lend a touch of color to salads.

DYEPLANT
Haematoxylon campechianum L. 76
(Caesalpiniaceae)

This tree, to 8 meters, has a greenish trunk branched from the base upward; it is armed with strong spines up to 1.5 cm in length. The leaves are composed of 4 to 8 obovate, 1 to 3 cm leaflets. The yellow flowers are grouped in showy, pendulous, axillary inflorescences; the fruits are curiously-shaped legumes up to 5 cm in length. The heartwood of this tree, which is spontaneous in the dry forests near the coasts in Central America and the Caribbean, provides man with haematoxylon, a natural coloring agent used in biological preparations and as a fabric dye; hence some of its many common names - for example, *Palo de tinta* and Dyeplant. Before the advent of synthetic dyes, this plant must have been of considerable economic value, especially if it is true, as it is believed to be, that the sole reason the British established their colony in the Honduras in 1638 was to gather and export the heavy and extremely hard wood (hence another of its common names, Logwood). *Haematoxylon* also possesses astringent properties and was used in the past for treating diarrhea and dysentery.

BARBADOS PRIDE
Caesalpinia pulcherrima (L.) Sw. 77
(Caesalpiniaceae)

C. pulcherrima (L.) Sw., also known as *Poinciana pulcherrima* L., is a small shrub to 5 meters with a sparse crown. The bipinnate leaves have 6 to 12 pairs of primary divisions, which are each divided into 3 to 9 pairs of leaflets. The petals of the beautiful flowers present marked chromatic variations, from deep red over the whole surface to red with bright yellow margins; not infrequently, myriad variations may be seen on a single plant. The fruits are pendulous legumes, 8 to 12 cm in length. The area of origin of this plant is unknown, even though it could reasonably be placed in Central America, where it is cultivated as an ornamental (for use in gardens, singly on lawns, or as hedging) and is also found growing spontaneously in the degraded coastal forests. A tea prepared with the flowers is used to alleviate menstrual cramps; the leaves are toxic.

CAESALPINIA VIOLACEA (MILL.) STANDL. 78
(NO COMMON ENGLISH NAME)
(Caesalpiniaceae)

Differently from *C. pulcherrima*, *C. violacea* is a tree to 10 meters.

78

species of the genus *Opuntia* are cultivated in the hot, dry regions of the world as crops or for their medicinal properties, and of some there exist many cultivars. The edible fruits can be cooked to produce an excellent jelly; the fermented juice yields a good alcoholic beverage. The stem segments can be used for preparing infusions that are efficacious in treating inflammations and ulcers; the flowers are utilized in treatment of diarrhea; the fruits are eaten raw as a cure for gonorrhea.

79

80 ▼

The bipinnate leaves have 2 to 4 pairs of primary divisions and 6 to 9 pairs of secondary divisions. The single leaflets are ovate to elliptical with acute tips, and leathery in consistency with evident veinings, above all on the upper side of the blade. The flowers are bright yellow with scattered reddish speckles; the fruit is a papery-membranous legume to 12 cm. *C. violacea* is native to the degraded scrub woods of Central America and the Caribbean.

Tuna
Opuntia dillenii
(Ker.-Gawl.) Haw. 79 80
(Cactaceae)

The genus *Opuntia* groups all of those plants commonly known as Prickly Pears or Indian Figs: more than two hundred species, all native to the Americas from Canada to Patagonia and all shrubs or small trees with jointed stems formed of rounded, flattened segments and leaves that have become tufts of bristles, spines, or hairs, depending on the species. *O. dillenii* grows spontaneously along the coasts of the Caribbean islands and south Florida; its strong spines, 2 to 5 cm in length, are grouped by threes to sevens. The flowers are yellow or orange, sometimes blushed red near the base. The fruits are purple. Although care must be taken during harvesting to avoid being wounded by the spines, many

81

It flourishes and propagates rapidly by vegetative reproduction as long as it is in full sun and conditions are dry, but at the first appearance of neighboring shrubs that block the light it tends to rapidly disappear. The sweet fruit is generally eaten raw, alone or in fruit salads. The spines can cause troublesome irritations.

NIGHT-BLOOMING CEREUS
Selenicereus grandiflorus (L.)
Britt. & Rose 83
(Cactaceae)

The genus name *Selenicereus*, also known as Moon Cactus, derives from the Greek word for moon (*selene*) and the Latin *cereus*, or wax candle: many members of this genus are, in fact, erect and columnar with large night-blooming flowers. The popular *S. grandiflorus* (Night-Blooming Cereus or Queen-of-the-Night) is a vining shrub with fleshy stems that grow to 5 meters in length, but since they are small in diameter (1 to 3 cm) they are so flaccid that they require the support of other plants. The stems are covered with silky spines up to 1.5 cm long and with deciduous whitish or yellow hairs. The flowers are white. *S. grandiflorus* is native to Jamaica, the Cayman Islands, and Cuba, where it inhabits the scrub woods near the coast, but is also grown as an ornamental in suitable climates and indoors in many countries and is also the subject of large-scale cultivation in greenhouses, since it yields a medicinal substance that stimulates the cardiovascular system.

MADAME YASS
Parkinsonia aculeata L. 81
(Fabaceae)

This slender tree to 10 meters, with a thin crown and general habit reminiscent of *Casuarina equisetifolia*, is native to tropical America. The compound leaves have 10 to 25 pairs of tiny leaflets and at the base one or two pairs of stipules that have become spines. The flowers, having one red and four yellow petals, never exceed 2 cm in length and are borne in groups at the ends of the outermost branches. The fruit is a brown, woody legume, 5 to 15 cm in length. On Haiti, this plant goes by the unusual name of Madame Yass.

TURK'S CAP
Melocactus intortus
(Mill.) Urban 82
(Cactaceae)

This ovoid cactus, from 60 to 80 cm tall, is completely covered by spines arranged in longitudinal rows and is distinguished by the cephalium typical of the genus: a woolly and bristly reddish cylindrical mass, which may be as large as 30 cm height by 8 cm diameter, topping the plant at maturity. The pink flowers develop among the bristles and spines in the apical portion of the cephalium. *M. intortus* grows in arid, rocky areas along the coasts of the Bahamas, Puerto Rico, and the Lesser Antilles, and is widely cultivated as an ornamental in many of the world's dry regions.

82

83 ▶

ANTHROPIZED ENVIRONMENTS

The anthropized environments of the Caribbean area host a number of quite peculiar species of flora.

Herbs, lianas, and small shrubs together often give rise, along the roadsides in the peri-urban areas, to a type of vegetation whose very existence depends on the continual disturbance typical of these environments. Many of the species are members of the Bindweed family (Convolvulaceae) of creeping herbs that do not seem at all affected by being trodden on - quite the contrary, in fact, since thanks to the capacity of any fragment of these plants to generate a new individual they can profit by the disturbance to reproduce.

85

BLOODFLOWER
Asclepias curassavica L. 84
(Asclepiadaceae)

An herb to 40 to 60 cm, usually unbranched. The opposite, lanceolate leaves, about 5 by 12 cm in size, are supported by a petiole measuring about one centimeter. The small flowers, with orange or light red petals around a bright yellow center (the stylar column), are grouped in inflorescences at the apex of the stem. Like other members of the Milkweed family, the Bloodflower is commonly found along the roadsides and in abandoned areas at low altitudes. All parts of the plant are toxic to man, but not to the Monarch butterfly, whose larvae appear to feed exclusively on the leaves of many species of Asclepiadaceae.

BLUE SNAKEWEED
Stachytarpheta jamaicensis (L.) M. Vahl 85
(Verbenaceae)

This herb grows to one meter in open areas and along the roadsides, with creeping stems that are, however, erect in the distal portion. The ovate-elliptical leaves are 2 by 7 cm in size, with dentate margins. The flowers, which range in color from violet to blue, open only a few at a time in erect inflorescences as

86

long as 20 cm. For more than two centuries, this herb has been a mainstay of folk medicine in treatment of dermal fungus infections, diarrhea, and diabetes, and as a laxative. It is also eaten raw as a salad green.

YELLOW VIGNA
Vigna luteola (Jacq.) Benth. 86
(Fabaceae)

This low, rarely climbing herb grows in the arid and disturbed areas of Central America. The leaflets of the trifoliate leaves are ovate and shorter than the petiole, with two ovate-lanceolate stipules at the base. The yellow flowers, up to 3 cm in diameter, may be solitary or grouped by twos, threes, or fours along an elongated axis. The legumes, which

88

at maturity are dark brown in color, measure from 4 to 8 cm in length but are no wider than 4 mm.

SHRUB VERBENA
Lantana camara L. 87
(Verbenaceae)

Although the genus *Lantana* is native to South America and western Africa, it has by now been introduced to all the tropical countries of the world and has become naturalized wherever climatic conditions permit. *L. camara* is a small shrub never over one meter in height, with erect herbaceous stems and opposite, lanceolate leaves that are rough to the touch. The small flowers, borne in congested terminal inflorescences on long stalks, vary in color from yellow

to orange to red, although there also exist cultivars in which they are white, pink, or lemon-yellow.

LEAD TREE
Leucaena leucocephala (Lam.) De Wit. 88
(Mimosaceae)

A small tree, native to Florida and California, that has become naturalized in many tropical-climate areas, where it prefers roadsides and disturbed habitats. The leaves are formed of 10 to 20 pairs of small linear leaflets. The flowers are very small, yellow, and grouped in globose inflorescences; the fruits are flattened legumes up to 20 cm in length and brown in color.

87

89

MORNING GLORY
Ipomoea fistulosa Mart. ex. Choisy 89 90
(Convolvulaceae)

The Caribbean region counts three quite common species of the herb genus *Ipomoea*. They are all creeping lianas or climbing herbs that seek support on the surrounding vegetation; the filmy leaves are generally wide and tending toward heart-shaped, with an elongated blade and a pointed tip. The very large flowers (10 to 15 cm diameter) have a funnel-shaped portion and a spreading corolla of a more or less deep pink color. Of the three species, *I. fistulosa*, which is spontaneous in the clearings of the coastal forests of Central America but also common along the roadsides, is that which most tends to climb

90

upward on trees and shrubs, or on walls, forming hedges. The common genus name of Morning Glory derives from the fact that the flowers tend to open only in the early hours of the morning and close during the hottest hours of the day.

91

MORNING GLORY
Ipomoea macrantha Roem. & Schult. 91
(Convolvulaceae)

The stems of this creeping herb, found in disturbed habitats in the coastal areas of all the tropical regions, grow as long as 12 meters. The leaves are darker green than those of *I. fistulosa*, and also blunter and wider at the base. The seeds are toxic and can cause hallucinations. The young leaves are edible if cooked. The plant yields a substance used in medicine to stimulate uterine contractions.

92

CRAB BUSH
Evolvulus squamosus
Britton [92]
(Convolvulaceae)

Although belonging to the Bindweed family, the Crab Bush possesses certain peculiar characteristics that distinguish it from the other plants of the family and indeed of its same genus. It is a small shrub with erect branches, sometimes elongated and trailing. The leaves are linear and so small in size (often reduced to small scales) as to fully justify the species epithet *squamosus* ('scaly'). The characteristic funnel-shaped flowers, generally white but also purple or blue, are the feature that permits assigning this species to the family Convolvulaceae.

TREE COTTON
Gossypium hirsutum L. var. *punctatum* (Schum.) J. B. Hutch., Silow & Stephens [93]
(Malvaceae)

The annual cultivars of *G. barbadense* and *G. hirsutum* are the two most important cotton crop plants cultivated in the Caribbean. Cotton is probably native to Central and South America, but since it has been cultivated since time immemorial it is difficult to pinpoint its exact place of origin. It is certain that the Arawaks cultivated the plant before the arrival of the Caribs, and that they used it for making clothing and blankets. The cotton fiber used by man is obtained from the seed hairs or filaments that envelop the seed of this plant and favor its dispersal by wind. *G. barbadense* (American Pima Cotton or *Cotton noir*) and *G. hirsutum* or Tree Cotton (Upland Cotton) differ as to habit, which is bushy in the first case and arboreal in the second, and the form of the floral bracts, which in the first species are almost entire and tapered and in the second edged with triangular teeth. *G. hirsutum* var. *punctatum* is a variety that while derived from the first, shrubby plants introduced to this area long ago has now become spontaneous and behaves like a ruderal species.

93

GARDENS

Exception made for occasional local phenomena such as hurricanes, earthquakes, volcanic eruptions, and periods of prolonged drought, the environmental conditions typical of the islands of the Caribbean Sea are generally highly favorable to cultivation of all sorts of plants. We may confidently say that there exist are no general limiting factors to cultivation and that the few restrictions that do exist regard only species that are intolerant of calcareous substrates of coral origin (typical of the islands) or of the salt-laden sea winds of the coastal areas. Thus, practically speaking and with few exceptions, it is possible to grow anything anywhere in the Caribbean; here, any plant can be trusted to develop to the best of its capacity and to produce beautiful foliage and flowers in the wild, in the forests and along the coasts, and also in 'captivity', in the gardens and urban flowerbeds.

The Caribbean is heir to a long tradition of gardening, rooted in the troubled history of the region; today, this tradition emerges mainly in the roadside plantings, the gardens of the hotels, the parks and other public spaces, and in the vegetable gardens and food-crop plantations.

Although there do exist differences, in terms of climate and geological substrate, among the various islands, there also exists a surprising uniformity as regards the species most commonly used as ornamentals in the urban and peri-urban areas. This is in large part due to the fact that many are exotic plants that have been imported to the Caribbean from all of the world's tropical-climate areas - plants which thanks to their beauty and originality attract the attention of the many visitors to these islands.

The first chapter in the gardening history of Caribbean should begin with a discussion of the use made of various plants by the first immigrant population to these lands: the Arawaks of North America, who Columbus described as being olive-skinned with fine, straight, black hair. A people who lived by farming and hunting, the Arawaks were for the most part vegetarians. They cultivated the pineapples and apricots of Santo Domingo (Hispaniola) and integrated their diets with the meat of the manatee, the tortoise, the iguana, and certain birds. They also cultivated cotton, for their clothing, and tobacco, which they preferred to chew rather than smoke. Their society was thus probably based essentially on a balance of farming and hunting, and it would seem that they were a fundamentally peaceful people.

This must have been more or less the way things stood when the Caribs, a warlike and decidedly less refined people, migrated into the area from the south. They were dark-skinned, with coarse, curly hair, and above all were of larger build - and possessed of a greater propensity for physical combat. Thanks to these characteristics, the Caribs soon achieved supremacy over the guileless and slighter Arawaks. Unlike the Arawaks, however, the Caribs were not good farmers; they migrated continually from one island to another aboard their well-made boats and they lived mainly by fishing and hunting. Nor, apparently, did they disdain cannibalism, as was reported by Diego Alvarez Chanca, the physician of the Spanish royal family assigned to Colum-

bus' second expedition of 1493-96 with, it would seem, the task of caring mainly for Columbus' enemies and the casualties among their number. The food of the Caribs was highly spiced with a sauce made of manioca and crushed chili peppers; they also made use of alcoholic beverages distilled from cassava (*Manihot esculenta*).

When the two societies came into direct collision, before Columbus' arrival in the West Indies, the Caribs killed many of the Arawak men, captured the women, and raised the children in accordance with their own customs: Arawak society and culture thus slowly but inexorably began to decline. The Caribs nevertheless learned some farming techniques from the Arawaks; their villages were all the better for it, and soon became true garden spots.

The many marvelous gardens are among the most striking elements in the already spectacular Caribbean environment.

Columbus described them as being ringed by kitchen gardens, with palms and maize plants, 'as pretty as those we see in Castile in the month of May'.

This was, then, the situation that greeted the arrival of the Spaniards. Columbus first made landfall in the Bahamas (San Salvador is the currently preferred site), but the first true Spanish village was built on Haiti, where Columbus took refuge following the destruction of his flagship, the *Santa Maria*. The Genoese explorer's second voyage marked the start of importation of 'exotic species' to the Caribbean, mainly in the form of the seeds of a number of European food crops: melons, watermelons, oranges, sugar cane, and others. The Europeans, however, found themselves hard pressed to work the land, due to the oppressive heat and high humidity; they thus conscripted natives as slaves. The Arawaks, on the one hand, were constitutional-ly unable to tolerate intensive labor, and the Caribs, on the other, proved to be far from passive subjects for domination - in fact, they preferred committing suicide and killing their children to living in slavery. There thus began a slow process of genocide, to which the Arawaks were the first to succumb: the few who had survived the passage of the Caribs were in practice exterminated by the Spaniards. The more belligerent Caribs instead attempted to oppose resistance, and in some cases even managed to capture large numbers of Europeans, who they either used as slaves - or ate. On some islands, only a few of the early colonists survived, and that thanks only to the stores laid in after the first harvests. But the European colonization voyages to the West Indies continued without pause and at an ever-quickening pace, and it was not long before the Caribs too had been exterminated.

The streets of the towns and cities are often verdant with palms and other plants.

was for a long time one of the most heavily traveled. Asian plants previously introduced to Africa and Europe reached the West Indies by the same route. The Tamarind was introduced to the island of Barbados in 1647, and in 1722, in his book *Nouveau Voyage aux Îles d'Amérique*, the Dominican friar Jean-Baptiste Labat wrote of a boulevard of these trees leading to a garden on the island, and of how their lush foliage provided pleasant shade for the homes along the way. Griffith Hughes, in his book *The Natural History of the Barbados* (1750), described the 'cabbage palms', presumably of the genus *Sabal*, that surrounded certain homes. But the cultivated plants served other uses than the purely ornamental: many species also produced edible fruits. H. N. Coleridge, in *Six Months in the West Indies* (1826), pointed out that while the slaves on the Barbados were not granted a percentage of the products of their labors, they were allowed to keep 'gardens of their own which they might cultivate as they please: either yams, Indian corn, plantains or even canes are to be seen around every hut'.

The economy of the West Indies was in any case supported entirely by slave labor, which by this time was exclusively African since the native Arawaks and Caribs had been exterminated by the Spaniards. During the American Revolution, the Caribbean islands were despoiled of their farm products to supply the armies engaged in battle, and consequently the slaves, lowest in the social hierarchy, were deprived of even the foodstuffs they needed to survive. This state of affairs sparked the slave revolt on what was then known as Saint Domingue on 24 August 1791; it was the prelude to country's independence from France, under the Arawak name of Haiti, in 1804. In this period, the production of sugar cane fell dramatically, with an ensuing mass exodus of the populations of the islands.

Despite these events, the eighteenth century was mostly one of relative calm, during which the plantation owners dedicated much time to building and embellishing their homes. Many began building stone houses, in the European fashion. Each owner had many slaves at his disposal, whom he employed in field work but also in caring for the open spaces around the plantation buildings, which became true gardens, in the English style, with broad lawns cut through by paths and avenues and planted with single trees and flowerbeds. The cities were also invested by this wave of innovation and acquired parks, tree-lined squares, and planted cemeteries, while the churches were ringed with elegant, colorful gardens. Janet Schaw, in her *Journal of a Lady of Quality*, includes a delightful description of a garden on Antigua: 'My bed-chamber, to render it more airy, has a door which opens into a parterre of flowers, that glow with colours, which only the western sun is able to raise into such richness, while every breeze is fragrant with perfumes that mock the poor imitations to be produced by art. This parterre is surrounded by a hedge of Pomegran-

Sugar cane, one of the plants that has had the greatest impact on the economic history of the Caribbean, was introduced to Spain from its native India and thence to the Canary Islands and later the Caribbean region, where as early as 1530 it had become the basis for a thriving industry. And if on the one hand sugar cane was for long time the sole basis for the economy of these islands, on the other, the fight for supremacy in this market was for the Caribbean the major cause of an interminable series of local conflicts when in the 17th century there began a long period of struggles between the Catholic and the Protestant or Anglican powers in Europe, led by Spain and England, respectively. The latter faction won out, in part thanks to the aid received from private enterprise and from the buccaneers Hawkins and Drake, who, secretly supported by the British crown, plied the Caribbean Sea preying on Spanish convoys and settlements. Already sorely tried by these continual raids, the Spanish monopoly on trade between Europe and the West Indies was further menaced by the Dutch merchant marine, which by the mid-1600s counted more than 800 ships in the Atlantic. In the end, however, the Dutch showed more interest in the slave trade than in establishing permanent colonies on the Caribbean islands, and therefore never entered into direct conflict with the other Europeans already settled there. The British government, instead, encouraged private citizen-colonists to take possession of lands in the region in order to be able to later claim them as British crown territories. Thus it was not long before the West Indies were transformed into checkerboards of farms that produced goods for the mother country, with great economic benefit also for the islands themselves, where the standard of living improved greatly. In 1655, the British general Robert Venables described how, in Santo Domingo, 'every night was borne a most delicious scent from the shore by the land wind as could possibly be smelt of the fruits, blossoms and herbs of the towne, there being many gardens joyning to the houses'.

Tropical plants, especially those of African origin, continued to be imported and planted, and in increasing quantities, since the Africa-Canary Islands-Caribbean route

ate, which is now loaded both with fruit and blossom...'. The squares and the avenues of the cities were planted with palms (*Roystonea regia*), poincianas (*Caesalpinia pulcherrima* and *Delonix regia*), and Lignum-vitae (*Guaiacum officinale*). During this same period, however, people began to realize just how much the islands depended on foreign trade, especially for their food supplies, and just how easy prey they were, during the periods of isolation caused by the various wars, to famine or shortages - which naturally weighed most heavily on the slaves. The Royal Society for the Encouragement of Arts, Manufactures, and Commerce (Royal Society of Arts, founded in 1754 by William Shipley) thus drafted a scheme for increasing the agricultural production of the New World British colonies, with cash incentives for those who cropped new plants in the West Indies. Olives, opium, cotton, vanilla, peppers, camphor, and an infinite variety of dye and ornamental plants were introduced, in the belief that the increase in production would have been sufficient to provide the needed food for the slaves.

The abolition of the slave trade and slavery in the British and French West Indies by the mid-19th century had extremely important repercussions on Caribbean society - comparable only to the effects of the introduction of sugar cane. By the end of the same century, slavery had been abolished in all the other colonies, and the reform of the social classes as a consequence of the Industrial Revolution further complicated matters. Generally speaking, the slaves were not prepared to run farms by themselves, and thus many continued to work as paid laborers on the large industrial plantations. Some did, however, choose free enterprise, but this proved to be plausible only on those which were at the time already the most productive of the islands, and furthermore involved importation of new food crop plants, like akee (*Blighia sapida*), breadfruit (*Artocarpus altilis*), jackfruit (*Artocarpus heterophyllus*), and mango (*Mangifera indica*). Slowly, however, the freed slaves created new farms and an innovative system for laying out the green spaces around their homes. In his book *The West Indies and the Spanish Main*, Anthony Trollope described the new situation: 'They are not filled, as a peasant's garden in England or in Ireland is filled, with potatos and cabbages, or other vegetables similarly uninteresting in their growth; but contain cocoa-trees, breadfruit trees, oranges, mangos, limes, plantains, jack-fruit, soursop, avocado, pears and a score of others, all of which are luxuriant trees, some of them of considerable size, and all of them of great beauty'. There were also bananas, cassava, sweet potatoes, maize, and other plants, and the cottage gardens boasted a variety of flowers, with Hibiscus bushes, Cassia, the Jumby Bead Bush (*Erythrina corallodendron*), the blue, white, and pink Convolvulus, and the Poinsettia (*Euphorbia pulcherrima*).

But sugar cane suffered another crisis and it consequently became necessary to introduce another spate of food crop plants. In order to keep track of all these new exotics, food crops and ornamentals alike, a network of botanical gardens was created under the direct supervision of the Royal Botanic Gardens, Kew. As part of this initiative, a Royal Commission directed by Sir Daniel Morris, Director of the Public Gardens and Plantations of Jamaica, was created and charged with individuating the most suitable agricultural and horticultural crops for the particular climatic conditions and soils of each island in the West Indies. In a report to the Horticultural Club of London, Morris described the gardens of the Caribbean: 'In point of scenery and displays of tropical vegetation, the islands of the Caribbean are among the most beautiful areas in the world. Their inherent fertility and their advantageous geographical position have at various times in history brought them great prosperity. They were once renowned for sugar, supplying close to the entire world's requirement for the crop. Later they became renowned for fruit, spices and other agricultural crops. When there are so many conditions favourable to the growth of plants, the task of the cultivator is to repress rather than to urge. He has to fight against tropical weeds with a persistency his northern brother can scarcely realize. Heavy downpours of rain and the fierce rays of the sun have to be equally borne, hence shrubs and trees are more in favour than herbaceous plants. Indeed delicate plants require the shelter of trees and rocks...'.

With all these conditions present in the Caribbean, the islands boast an extremely rich variety of spontaneous flora and a just as abundant array of exotic plants, introduced during the various stages of the complex and troubled social and economic history of the area. It is to the historical domestic demand for exotic species to diversify production on the islands that we owe the singular potpourri of cultivated flora found in the Caribbean today. Wherever visitors to the islands stop, they will always be greeted by the sight of beautiful plants, grown both as food crops and for purely ornamental reasons. Visiting the gardens of the Caribbean has become a popular pastime - and sometimes even the main reason for making a trip to the Caribbean. The most important of the exotic plants one may find in the gardens, parks, and various other man-made green areas in the Caribbean islands are listed and described below in alphabetical order by scientific name.

The lush Caribbean flora reigns supreme even at the edges of pools and patios.

94

95

97

96

CHENILLE PLANT
Acalypha hispida Burm. f. 94
(Euphorbiaceae)

The genus *Acalypha* is native to
Southeast Asia and the Pacific region.
Its members are generally erect
shrubs to 5 meters, even though the
stems are herbaceous. The alternate
leaves, borne on variable-length
petioles, are strikingly maculated in
various colors, from bright green to
the more or less deep purples (hence
the common genus names Jacob's
Coat and Match-Me-If-You-Can). The
nature of the variegation of the leaves
is especially important in the
cultivars derived from *A. tricolor*
Seem., whose leaves may be green,
green and white, green and yellow,
bronze, copper-colored, or varying

shades of brown, from light to dark.
The leaves of *A. hispida* are generally
green, but this species is selected on
the basis of the length and the
persistence of the long pendulous
inflorescence, generally rust red in
color, from which it takes its
common names of Chenille Plant
and Red Hot Cattail.

IMPALA LILY
Adenium obesum (Forssk.) Roem.
& Schult. ssp *obesum* 96
(Apocynaceae)
Adenium obesum ssp *swazicum*
(Stapf.) G. Rowley 97
(Apocynaceae)

A shrub with a succulent trunk no
taller than one meter, native to the

desert regions of the Arabian
peninsula and of eastern Africa;
hence the common genus name of
Desert Rose. The trunk is typically
engrossed and light grey in color,
while the leaves are glossy dark
green. The trumpet-shaped flowers
vary in color from pink to deep red.
This species is eminently suited for
planting in rock gardens. The
exudates from the trunk are
extremely toxic.

COMMON ALLAMANDA
Allamanda cathartica L. 95
(Apocynaceae)

A small vine-like shrub, native to
Brazil, the young branches of which
are not completely lignified and
therefore pendulous. The persistent
opposite leaves are thick, dark green
in color, and covered with a layer of
shiny wax. The yellow flowers are
trumpet-shaped, fused into a tube

and lobed and spreading at the top. Flowering is staggered: the plant will always have one or more open flowers. There also exist varieties with double the number of petals. The Brazilian *Allamanda blanchetii* A. DC. in DC. is in all respects similar to *A. cathartica* L., differing only in having violet instead of yellow flowers; this species must not be mistaken for *Cryptostegia grandiflora*, sometimes called Purple Allamanda, from which it differs in not having latex in its stems. As the name suggests, *A. cathartica* L. is used in medicine as a cathartic or purgative.

RED GINGER
Alpinia purpurata (Vieill.) Schum. [98]
(Zingiberaceae)

The Red Ginger, spontaneous in the Pacific islands, is a perennial herb to 5 meters, with alternate, light green leaves borne along the entire length of the stem. The leaf blade, 10 to 15 cm wide, may be as long as 80 cm, with central yellowish-green veining. The small flowers, which are grouped in a dense, erect inflorescence 20 to 35 cm in length, are whitish in color and enclosed by red-purple bracts, a peculiarity that determines the plant's high value as an ornamental. The species of the genus *Alpinia*, like others of the family Zingiberaceae, have parallel rather than pinnately-arranged veins and are thus easy to distinguish from other monocotyledons.

PINEAPPLE
Ananas bracteatus (Lindl.) Schult. f. 'Striatus' [99]
(Bromeliaceae)

The Pineapple, although native to Brazil, had already been introduced to the island of Guadalupe when Columbus arrived there in late 1493, on his second voyage to the West Indies. The genus name *Ananas* derives from the local term *a' nanas*, meaning 'good-tasting plant', but since its fruit much resembles a pinecone, it soon came to be known as *piña* to the Spaniards and pine-apple to the English. Columbus imported the plant to Spain, and its fruit quickly became a favorite among the Europeans; its diffusion was so rapid that by 1548 it was cultivated on Madagascar and by 1590 in India. The Pineapple is a perennial herb with a basal rosette of leaves up to one meter in length with spiny-toothed margins and varying in color from a more or less brilliant green to reddish. A scape, arising from the rosette and generally to 50 cm, bears a terminal inflorescence made up of numerous red-violet flowers. The fruit is undoubtedly the most characteristic part of the plant: it is actually an infructescence (that is, a group of many fruits - up to two hundred - fused together) topped by a crown of spiny pointed leaves; in the 'Honey-Gold' cultivar, this multiple fruit may weigh up to 7 kilograms. The Pineapple is cultivated for its fruits, which are eaten in practically all parts of the world, and also for the important proteolytic enzyme it yields. The plant is also used as an ornamental in virtue of the beauty of both its leaves and its flowers, and many cultivars exist, including the 'Striatus' shown here, selected for the peerless striations of its leaves.

98

99

Breadfruit
Artocarpus altilis
(Parkinson) Fosb. [100]
(Moraceae)

Although most people know the legendary story of the mutiny on the HMS *Bounty*, led by Christian Fletcher, what is not as well known is the real scope of mission set for the *Bounty* and its crew. Captain William Bligh was sent to Tahiti in late 1788 by Joseph Banks, the botanist who had earlier accompanied James Cook on his expeditions to Asia, to collect the seeds of the Breadfruit tree, native to Southeast Asia and still today a major food source for the populations of the Pacific area, and carry them to the British colonies in the West Indies - with the aim of providing a good local source of food for the African slaves there. The mutiny of course prevented the captain from completing his mission; set adrift on a lifeboat, Bligh nevertheless managed to return to England, where in 1792 he organized a new voyage to Tahiti and finally did transport the seeds to the West Indies. The plant was successfully established by the English colonists, but it failed to live up to expectations since the slaves much preferred bananas, yucca, and other foodstuffs. The Breadfruit is a tree to 25 meters with more or less deeply lobed, leathery leaves up to 90 cm wide. The male flowers are small and are grouped in pendulous catkins, while the female flowers form large rounded inflorescences. The fruit grows to 30 cm in length and can weigh

100

more than 4 kilograms: it is rich in vitamins (A, B, and C) and starch, and is used much like a sweet-potato or plantain, even though it must be peeled and cooked before use. The cultivated variety is seedless. Another species of the same genus, *A. heterophyllus* Lam. (known by the common name of Jackfruit), is also cultivated for its fruit, although less commonly. It differs from the Breadfruit in having entire and smaller leaves (not exceeding 7 cm), and fruits borne directly on the stem of the plant; the fruits themselves are also much larger: up to 70 cm in length and weighing as much as 18 kilograms.

101

Orchid Tree
Bauhinia variegata L. [101]
(Caesalpiniaceae)

This deciduous tree, native to India, grows to 10 meters with a wide-spreading but relatively sparse crown. The even-pinnate compound leaves have lanceolate leaflets. *B. variegata* is commonly called the Orchid Tree, since the beautiful magenta flowers, streaked with purple and white and up to 12 cm in diameter, are grouped at the apices of the smaller branches in lateral inflorescences that recall those of the tropical orchids. The cultivars of this quite valuable ornamental differ as to the variegation of the flowers. The distinctive form of the crown makes the tree suitable for planting along roadsides; what is more, like the majority of the species of the family Caesalpiniaceae, *B. variegata* has no special soil requirements and grows rapidly. The bark contains great quantities of tannin and is used in the dyeing industry; in India, both the leaves and the flower buds are eaten.

STAR LEAF BEGONIA
Begonia heracleifolia Cham. & Schldl. [102]
(Begoniaceae)

The begonias are typically grown in hothouse conditions, but are also often used outdoors in rock gardens, especially in protected enclosures and in rocky borders around fountains or artificial pools in areas not exposed to full sunlight.
In these conditions, the begonias provide a year-round ground cover that is quite pleasing to the eye due to the large, variegated leaves, like those of *B. heracleifolia*, which vary from green to bronze in color.

AKEE
Blighia sapida Koenig. [103]
(Sapindaceae)

This species is named after the captain of the ill-fated HMS *Bounty*, William Bligh. It is a small

102

tree to 14 meters, with alternate, persistent, compound leaves with 3 to 5 pairs of opposite, elliptical leaflets. The white flowers are small and borne in elongated inflorescences. The fruits are globose, about 5 cm in diameter, and divided internally into three locules that open at maturity; each of the three sections contains one shiny black seed, about 1 cm in diameter, surmounted by a whitish fleshy excrescence 2 to 3 cm im length. This outgrowth, which is called an aril, or *akee* from the African name of the plant, is quite flavorful and is commonly eaten in the West Indies as a fruit. The plant is native to tropical Africa; it was introduced to the Caribbean aboard the slave galleys. Immature green arils and all the other parts of the plant are extremely toxic and cause what is known as 'Jamaica sickness': severe hypoglycemia that can lead to death. For this reason, *B. sapida* should never be planted in areas accessible to children.

103

105

BOUGAINVILLEA
Bougainvillaea spectabilis Willd. 104 105
(Nyctaginaceae)

The Bougainvillea bears the name of the French navigator Louis de Bougainville, who visited Brazil in the 18th century and who first introduced the plant to Europe for cultivation. The species of this genus are woody climbers, with (sometimes hooked) spines along the stems that permit them to cling to various types of supports; they are therefore often and very successfully used for embellishing partitions such as trellises. The acuminate, glabrous leaves, up to 20 cm in length, are lighter on the undersurface. The flowers are so small as to be almost invisible; the function of attracting pollinating insects is instead carried out by the calyx, which is yellow or red in color, and three bracts of the same color, similar in shape to the leaves, subtending the flowers. The Bougainvillea grows rapidly and flowers all year round, reasons for which it has long been cultivated and has spawned many cultivars. There therefore exist a great number of varieties of this species, with differing growth forms, from scandent shrubs to trailers, and bracts of many different shades.

GUARNACO
Brownea sp. 106
(Caesalpiniaceae)

The genus *Brownea* is made up of shrubs or medium-to-small trees, native to tropical America. They are widely used as ornamental plants thanks to their showy inflorescences, which vary in color from red to orange and are borne directly on the trunk. *B. grandiceps* Jacq., also known as the Rose of Venezuela, is the species with

◀104

the largest inflorescences, although those of *B. coccinea* Jacq., known commonly as Flame Bean and again from Venezuela, run a very close second.

POWDER PUFF TREE
Calliandra haematocephala Hassk. 107
(Mimosaceae)

This small tree, with its heavy, rounded crown, is native to Bolivia. Its prize feature is its singular inflorescence: a globose mass of red formed by the stamens of the flowers, flecked with smaller darker spots - the anthers. The different species of the genus *Calliandra* each have flowers of a different color: various shades of red, pink, or white.

106

107

WEEPING BOTTLEBRUSH
Callistemon viminalis
(Sol. ex Gaertn.)
G. Don ex Loud. [108]
(Myrtaceae)

The Weeping Bottlebrush is a large bush or small tree growing to 5 to 6 meters, with a dense crown made up of flexuous or vimineous branches - hence the species epithet *viminalis* - like those of the Osier (*Salix viminalis*) used for weaving baskets. When young, the branches are covered with silky hairs. The alternate leaves are lanceolate in form. The genus name *Callistemon* means 'beautiful stamens' (from the Greek *kalos* = beautiful and *stemon* = warp or thread, hence stamen) and in fact this feature is typical of many Myrtaceae. The flowers, reduced to the bright red stamens and yellowish anthers, are borne in thick, pendulous heads that resemble bottle-brushes. The fantastical shape and color of the inflorescences make this plant a natural as an ornamental. The different species of *Callistemon*, all native to Australia, tend to cross easily, and although this characteristic often makes certain identification difficult, it has been widely exploited by man to produce cultivars.

108

109

110

APPLE OF SODOM
Calotropsis procera (Aiton)
Aiton f. [109]
(Asclepiadaceae)

This shrub, resembling a tree in its habit, grows to 5 meters with a stout, smooth stem, branches that are white-tomentose when young, and fleshy leaves, 10 to 20 cm wide, velvety-tomentose when young but tending to become glabrescent with age. Both the branches and the leaves produce considerable quantities of a milky, poisonous exudate. The plant flowers from May through November; the corolla, about 20 cm across, is white at the center and greenish toward the outside, with purple petal tips. The large, round fruits, resembling apples, are filled with light, feathery seeds; it is to the fruits that we probably owe one of the common names of this plant, Apple of Sodom. *C. procera* is native to Africa and western Asia; it is cultivated as an ornamental but tends to become naturalized, especially along roadsides.

NATAL PLUM
Carissa macrocarpa (Ecklon)
A. DC. [110]
(Apocynaceae)

C. macrocarpa is a shrub native to South Africa that bears its leaves crowded onto the terminal portion of the branches. The leaves are opposite and shiny green and

leathery, with prominent veins and a distinctive small spine at the tip of each. The plant is often used for hedging, which thanks to the leaf spines becomes an impenetrable barrier. The strongly fragrant flowers, which may be as large as 5 cm diameter, are made up of 5 linear-lanceolate snow-white petals. *C. macrocarpa* is one of the rare exceptions to the rule that all plants secreting milky exudates, like the majority of the Euphorbiaceae and many species classified as Apocynaceae (to which family the genus *Carissa* belongs), must be considered highly toxic. The fruits of *C. macrocarpa* or Natal Plum are in fact edible and are used in making jams and jellies.

BAG FLOWER
Clerodendrum splendens
G. Don ex James [111]
(Verbenaceae)

Like *C. thomsoniae*, *C. splendens* is a climbing shrub that grows spontaneously in southern Africa. Although its overall structure is similar to that of the other climbing clerodendrons, *C. splendens* differs from *C. thomsoniae* in having darker green and decidedly larger leaves, and smaller flowers in which the calyx, corolla and stamens are all with bright red, grouped in heavy inflorescences the stalks of which are also red. A light red cultivar, called 'Guardia Civil', is cultivated on Puerto Rico.

BLEEDING HEART VINE
Clerodendrum thomsoniae
Balf. f. [112]
(Verbenaceae)

The common name of Bleeding Heart
Vine derives from the peculiar shape
and color of the calyx of the flowers
of this climbing shrub. The opposite,
long-stalked leaves have wide
elliptical blades and an upper surface
that is decidedly rough to the touch.
The singular flowers have a calyx
formed of five sepals fused to form a
five-cornered structure with five
heart-shaped faces; the tube-like
corolla projects beyond the calyx, but
is in turn outstripped in length by the
stamens. The persistent calyx is
creamy yellow in color, while the
early-falling corolla is red and the
stamens are whitish with red anthers.
The single flowers are grouped in
rich, pendulous inflorescences. There
exist many garden varieties of this

112

113

species, which is native to the
tropical-climate areas of southern
Africa.

BUTTERCUP TREE
Cochlospermum vitifolium
(Willd.) Spreng. [113]
(Cochlospermaceae)

The ornamental potential of this
species, a tree to 15 meters native to
tropical America, is expressed to the
full during the dry season, when, after
it has shed its leaves in response to
the diminished availability of water
(and consequent need to limit
evaporation of remaining moisture),
its flowering time begins. Thus, in just
a short time, the whole aspect of the
plant changes completely, the green
of the leaves being replaced by the
yellow or yellow-orange of the
flowers. What is more, the petals do
not lose their color once they have
fallen, so the ground around the plant
seems painted orange for the entire
dry season.

VARIEGATED LAUREL
Codiaeum variegatum
(L.) Bl. [114] [115]
(Euphorbiaceae)

This evergreen shrub is native to the
Moluccas and to Malaysia, where it is
put to use by the native populations
for producing clothing and as a
medicinal plant. Its variegated leaves
make it a common indoor ornamental
in other countries. The leaves, in fact,

114 ▲   115 ▼

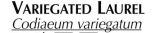

116

117

especially noteworthy when in blossom with its small, whitish flowers - which although in and of themselves insignificant are each subtended by three petal-like pink bracts covered with a thick silvery down, and grouped in elongated pendulous terminal inflorescences. Its common names include Wooly Congea and Shower of Orchids Vine.

ANCANHUITA
Cordia boissieri A. DC. 118
(Boraginaceae)

This species differs from *Cordia sebestena* mainly as regards its flowers, which are larger and creamy white in color, and its leaves, which while hairy are velvety to the touch. The plant is native to Mexico, but is often cultivated in the tropical areas of Central America.

118

vary greatly as to size but mainly as to color - which may be solid or streaked in combinations of green, yellow, white, orange, pink, red, crimson, and purple. The process of domestication, which has ended in this species' now being found in the gardens of tropical-climate regions around the world, has been long and involved. Some recent studies tell us that the plants originally cultured had solid green leaves, like those of the plants now classified as C. *mollucanum* Decne. By the early 19th century, the first cultivated varieties with yellow-streaked leaves had been produced, probably in Europe; we owe the great diversity of

the cultured forms now existing above all to work by French and Belgian horticulturists. From Europe, the many horticultural varieties that now go by the name of Variegated Laurel were introduced to all the tropical-climate regions of the world, including the area of origin of the species. *C. variegatum* reached the Caribbean only in the early 20th century.

WOOLY CONGEA
Congea tomentosa Roxb. 116 117
(Verbenaceae)

C. tomentosa is native to Thailand and Burma. It is a beautiful vine,

119

120

5-7 cm and in *C. malortieanus*, native to Central and South America, obovate-elliptical and about 20 by 18 cm. The flowers of these two species of *Costus* differ slightly in size and color: in *C. lucanusianus*, the tube is 2 cm long and white in color, while the petals are always white, with reddish borders edges and yellowish internally, 2.5 cm in length and up to 5 cm wide; in *C. malortieanus*, the tube is the same length (2 cm) but golden yellow in color and the petals, 5 by 5 cm in size, are yellow with red or brownish striations.

CANNONBALL TREE
Couroupita guianensis Aubl. 121
(Lecythidiaceae)

This large tree (to 35 to 40 meters), native to northern South America, has a narrow and only slightly branched crown; the simple leaves are wide with very short petioles. The flowers vary in color from creamy yellow to pale pink and are borne in very long inflorescences on tangled stalks that branch out directly from the trunk, especially in the

SPIRAL GINGER
Costus malortieanus A. Wendl. 119
(Costaceae)

SPIRAL FLAG
Costus lucanusianus A. Braun & Schum. 120
(Costaceae)

The genus *Costus* counts about one hundred species in a distribution area covering the tropical-climate zones of Asia, Africa, and the Americas. Certain of these species are widely cultivated, for different reasons: for example, *C. lucanusianus* for its flowers and *C. malortieanus* for its leaves. Both are rhizomatous herbs with fleshy leaves, which in the west African native *C. lucanusianus* are oblong-lanceolate and 12-25 by

121

portion nearest the ground. The most distinctive feature of this plant is without a doubt its bizarre fruits, called cannonballs (hence the common names *Bala de Canon* in Spanish and Cannonball Tree in English), a sort of brown coconut about 20 cm in diameter. It generally takes about nine months for a cannonball to ripen, and as the fruiting process proceeds from the proximal to the distal portion of the inflorescence it is not uncommon to see ripe fruits near the trunk while there are still flowers in bloom at the apex of the inflorescence. The Cannonball Tree is not commonly planted in private gardens, but it is a frequent sight in many parks, for example on Puerto Rico, St Croix, and St Thomas, and an attraction in the botanical gardens of the region.

122

MILK AND WINE LILY
Crinum zeylanicum L. 122
(Amaryllidaceae)

The genus name *Crinum* derives from the Greek *krinon* = lily. *C. zeylanicum*, native to Asia and tropical Africa, is a herbaceous plant with lanceolate leaves up to 2 meters in length. The fragrant flowers, generally five to ten, are borne on an axis just a little shorter than the leaves. The three sepals and three petals are all linear and snow-white in color, sometimes streaked pink. This lily is cultivated in damp areas and is resistant to the sea winds.

123

MADAGASCAR RUBBER VINE
Cryptostegia grandiflora R. Br. 123
(Asclepiadaceae)

This vining shrub has opposite leaves that are a deep green in color, shiny, and leathery in consistency. The flowers are campanulate, up to 10 cm wide at the mouth, and pink to violet in color. The fruits are composed of two opposite excrescences, similar to legumes, borne at the apices of the branches. *C. grandiflora* is very similar to *Allamanda blanchetii*, from which it is, however, readily distinguished by its fruit and by the latex contained in its stem. The plant is native to central Africa and Madagascar, but since its latex is excellent for the production of rubber, it is widely cultivated - in fact, the Madagascar Rubber Vine is among the world's five most commonly used plants for this purpose.

ANGEL'S TRUMPET
Datura candida (Pers.) Stapf. 124
(Solanaceae)

D. candida (sometimes indicated as *Brugmansia candida* Pers.), is a tree to 7 to 8 meters, native to South America, that is commonly known as the Angel's Trumpet due to the peculiar form of the flowers. These are pendent from the crown of the tree (the Hawaiian name, *Nana-honau*, means 'earth-gazing') and formed of five off-white petals, fused for most of their length to form a tube 25 to 30 cm long and then opening out into a fluted bell with recurved apices. The alternate leaves, borne on long petioles, are velvety and up to 50 cm long. In this striking ornamental, the luminous color of the flowers, which are generally many in number, contrasts pleasingly with the dark green of the crown foliage.

124

TIGER'S CLAW
Erythrina variegata L. 125 126
(Fabaceae)

The Tiger's Claw is a tree to
15 meters with light green,
vertically striated bark and series of
very small blackish spines arranged
along the trunk. The leaves are
made up of three broadly ovate or
delta-shaped leaflets. The bright
scarlet red flowers are grouped in
dense inflorescences projecting
nearly horizontally from the
branches. The fruit is a brown,
typically nodulose legume about
20 cm in length. Although native to
tropical Africa, this species is
widely cultivated and tends to

become spontaneous along seasonal
watercourses. The species epithet
variegata refers to the variegations
of both the leaves and the flowers.

125 ▲   126 ▼

CROWN OF THORNS
Euphorbia milii Desmoul. var. *splendens* (Bojer ex Hook.) Ursch & Leandri 127
(Euphorbiaceae)

This is an erect shrub to 2 meters,
with stems that sometimes tend to
climb. The square or pentangular
stems are succulent and irregularly
branched and bear straight spines
sometimes reaching 4 cm. The
sparse leaves are small (at most,
5 cm) and obovate; the cauline
leaves tend to group in pseudo-
rosettes. The small but brightly-
colored flowers are arranged in the
inflorescences common to all
members of the family
Euphorbiaceae - umbel-like clusters
known as cyathia. The flowers have
neither petals nor sepals; the
function of attracting pollinating
insects (and users of the plant as an
ornamental) is assured by the
generally brightly-colored bracts at
the base of the single inflorescences.
In the case of *E. milii* var. *splendens*,
native to Madagascar, both the
bracts and the flower stalks are
reddish in color. Legend suggests
that the bracts were white until the
stems of the plant, with their long,
straight spines, were worn by Christ
- whereupon they became red and
the plant earned its common name
of Crown of Thorns.

127

128

129

POINSETTIA
Euphorbia pulcherrima
Willd. ex Klotzsch. 128
(Euphorbiaceae)

The Poinsettia is perhaps the best-known *Euphorbia* in the world, even though few people are aware that it is actually a member of this genus. This shrub has slender, sparse branches reaching no higher than 4 meters, and dark green, deciduous leaves, which may be as long as 32 cm. The inflorescence exhibits all the characteristics typical of the other members of the family Euphorbiaceae; in this case the bracts are identical in form to the leaves but a lovely light red in color. There exist many cultivars with bracts of varying shades of red. The plant can be cultivated in pots, and during the winter season is commonly used to lend a note of color to our homes.

MILKBUSH
Euphorbia tirucalli L. 129
(Euphorbiaceae)

The importance of *E. tirucalli* as an ornamental derives not from its flowers, which are small and insignificant, nor from its leaves, seeing as it has none worth mentioning, but instead from the fact that the green branches (which take over the photosynthesizing function of the tiny, early-caducous leaves) form twisted, tangled masses, creating barriers so dense as to be impenetrable. It is easy to recognize due to its being leafless and also flowerless for most of the year, but also on account of its latex, which in this species is caustic and very dangerous if ingested. The tree is native to the semidesert regions of South Africa; in the Caribbean islands it is called *antena* or *esqueleto* in Spanish and Milkbush, Pencil Tree, or Finger Tree in English.

GOLD SHOWER THRYALLIS
Galphimia glauca Cav. 130
(Malpighiaceae)

The genus *Galphimia* is remarkably similar to *Malpighia*, from which its name derives by anagram. *G. glauca*, native to Mexico and Guatemala, is a shrub to 4 meters with opposite, elliptical, light-green leaves. The yellow flowers, 2 to 3 cm wide, are borne in terminal inflorescences.

130

132

GARDENIA
Gardenia tahitensis DC. [132]
(Rubiaceae)

This is a shrub growing no taller than 5 meters, with opposite, verticillate, elliptical leaves that are shiny dark green and leathery, with evident veinings. The solitary flowers, formed of five to nine snow-white petals, have a tubular portion 2 to 3 cm in length and a spreading portion 5 to 8 cm wide. This species is native to the islands of the South Pacific but is frequently encountered on the Caribbean islands as well, where it is widely used as a hedge-forming shrub.

FALSE BIRD-OF-PARADISE
Heliconia sp. [131] [133] [134] [135]
(Heliconiaceae)

Heliconia, the sole genus in the family Heliconiaceae, counts about one hundred wild species distributed in the tropical-climate regions of the Americas, in Asia, and in the Pacific islands. There exist an 'infinite' number of hybrids and horticultural varieties: just think that in recent years alone the Thai gardeners have succeeded in producing ten or so new cultivars by hybridization; at the same time, new species have been discovered in the Brazilian jungles. The most recent revision of this group, carried out in 1991, is thus already hopelessly out of date - and in fact, as of 2000 a new census was being prepared.
On the basis of general habit, the species of the genus *Heliconia* may

◀ 131

be divided into three broad groupings: banana-type, cane-type, and ginger-type. The plants illustrated here are all species of the first type: herbs in which the stem is constituted by the leaf sheaths that roll up around each other to form a pseudo-stem of a certain bulk, as happens in other large-size monocotyledons like bananas and members of the genus *Strelitzia*, for which they may be mistaken - at least when only the vegetative part of the plant is considered. The petiole is elongated and the leaf blade is spatulate, rolled up in the gemma, and with evident central veining. The different forms of *Heliconia* derive mainly from crosses among species found in nature in the Caribbean islands, like *H. caribaea*

Lam. and *H. bihai* (L.) L., or with other species that grow spontaneously in the various regions of Central and South America. The cultivated forms are grown for their inflorescences subtended by beautifully colored and unusually shaped bracts. The exceptional flowers of the so-called False Bird-of-Paradise are highly-colored and waxy in consistency; the forms derived from *H. caribaea* Lam. and *H. bihai* (L.) L. are especially valuable commercially as cut flowers. All the species of *Heliconia* produce abundant nectar at the base of the bracts. Those species with erect inflorescences and broad bracts can hold large quantities of water and so create peculiar stagnant-water micro-environments in which multitudes of tiny aquatic animals live.

133

134

135

CHINA ROSE
Hibiscus rosa-sinensis L. [136] [137]
(Malvaceae)

The genus *Hibiscus* counts about 220 species originating in Asia and tropical Africa, among which are some of the world's most beautiful ornamental plants, all with splendid flowers. *H. rosa-sinensis* L., *H. syriacus* L. and *H. moscheutos* L. are the members of the genus preferred by the nurseries, due to the great variety of flower colors and leaf forms - and these elements are exploited, through successive hybridizations, to obtain even greater diversity. The assortment of cultivars derived from these species is thus immense, and immensely varied. *H. rosa-sinensis* L. (the China Rose, which also goes by a myriad of other common names), spontaneous in much of tropical and subtropical Asia, is a shrub to 4 meters; the shiny green leaves are oval or broadly lanceolate, toothed above all in the apical area, and up to 15 cm in length. The tubular campanulate flowers, which may be as wide as 25 cm diameter, vary greatly in color but are generally a red of varying intensity, darker in the internal basal portion. The plant flowers year-round.

136

137

138

JAPANESE HIBISCUS
Hibiscus schizopetalus
(Mast.) Hook. f. [138]
(Malvaceae)

This weeping shrub, to 3 meters, is native to east-central Africa. The branches are slender and scandent; the ovate leaves as long as 12 cm. The pendent pink or red flowers, with petals as long as 17 cm, are borne on long stalks. *H. schizopetalus* differs from *H. rosa-sinensis* and the cultivars derived from it for its deeply lobed or split petals - hence the species epithet. This species is probably a variant of *H. rosa-sinensis*, with which it readily hybridizes.

JASMINE
Jasminum pubescens Willd. [139]
(Oleaceae)
Jasminum nitidum Skan. [140]
(Oleaceae)

J. nitidum e *J. pubescens* are evergreen lianas native to tropical Asia but widely cultivated in all the tropical-climate regions of the world for their beautiful and intensely fragrant white flowers. The two species differ in their leaves, which while being entire, opposite, and lanceolate in both are shiny in *J. nitidum* and matte-surfaced in *J. pubescens*, and in the petals of the flowers, which are linear and more than eight in number in *J. nitidum* and lanceolate and from 4 to 9 in number in *J. pubescens*. *Jasminum officinale* is another

139

140

tubular portion is enveloped in heart-shaped, brightly-colored bracts varying in hue from red to purple and even yellow. The flowers are arranged in dense spiciform inflorescences borne at the ends of the branches. This plant is native to Central America, probably Mexico, but is today cultivated in the flowerbeds of many gardens.

MANGO
Mangifera indica L. [142]
(Anacardiaceae)

The Mango is a tree at times exceeding 30 meters in height, with a spreading, round crown. The shiny, lanceolate leaves, 30 by 8 cm, have prominent veins, especially on the underside, and are grouped in clusters at the ends of the branches. The Mango produces flowers and fruits all year round in different 'sectors' of the plant. The flowers are small and insignificant, arranged in pendent inflorescences up to 22 cm long. The green, oval fruits, ripening purple-brown or yellowish depending on variety, have very sweet yellow to orange flesh; they are eaten as is or used to produce juice or jams and jellies. The Mango is a member of the same family as Poison Ivy and Poison Sumac, and for this reason any part of the plant or fruit may cause a reaction in particularly sensitive subjects. *M. indica* is one of the oldest fruits used by man, since its cultivation probably began about 4000 years ago in Southeast Asia, the area to which it is native. Today, it is cultivated in many tropical countries, where its economic importance is often second only to that of the banana.

141 ▲   142 ▼

species cultivated in the Caribbean; it differs from the other two mentioned in having compound leaves with 5 to 9 leaflets and flowers with 4 to 5 ovate petals.

MEXICAN SHRIMP PLANT
Justicia brandegeana
Wassh. & L. B. Sm. [141]
(Acanthaceae)

A small shrub with erect, herbaceous branches and opposite, elliptical-lanceolate leaves on very short petioles. The leaf blade is rough to the touch and has slightly undulated margins. The distal portion of the pinkish to white tubular flowers is made up of five prominent lobes, of which the upper two are fused to form a hood. The

143

144

145

INDIAN MULBERRY
Morinda citrifolia L. 143
(Rubiaceae)

The genus *Morinda* counts eighty species distributed throughout the tropical-climate regions, where they are also the subject of large-scale cultivation. *M. citrifolia*, or Indian Mulberry, is a small tree to 6 meters height with an irregular crown and strong, dark grey leaves, sometimes as large as 25 by 12 cm, arranged in clusters at the ends of the branches together with the tenuous white blossoms, which develop into pulpy aggregate fruits similar to strawberries but whitish in color. Native to tropical Asia, this plant has become naturalized in vast areas of the Americas. The leaves are used to prepare poultices for treating arthritis and sores; the juice is widely sold as a tonic.

INDIAN MULBERRY
Morinda umbellata L. 144
(Rubiaceae)

M. umbellata, sometimes called *M. rojoc* hort., is also native to tropical Asia. It is an erect or climbing shrub to 5 meters, with leaves that with respect to those of

M. citrifolia are smaller, never exceeding 10 by 5 cm. The fruit is also smaller; the flowers, instead, are somewhat larger.

BANANA
Musa x paradisiaca L. 145
(Musaceae)

A gigantic herb to 8 meters whose leaves spring from a creeping rhizome; the leaf sheaths fuse to form a false trunk. The leaves have a broad blade, up to 2.3 meters in length, with prominent, reddish, central veining. The unisexual

flowers are arranged in spiciform inflorescences enveloped by bracts. The male flowers are found above; the females below. The spike bends down to form the axis that supports the clusters or 'hands' of individual fruits, the well-known bananas, which may be up to 9 cm in length in the wild form. The genus *Musa* is native to southwestern Asia, but its members are commonly cultivated all over the world wherever the climate permits. *M. x paradisiaca* is of great economic importance: it was the basis of the diet of the slaves deported to the Caribbean, and is still a staple foodstuff in many poorer countries. It is also a prized ornamental, and thus the various cultivars tend to favor either high yields for production as a food crop or development of new forms for use as decorative elements in outdoor spaces.

OLEANDER
Nerium oleander L. [146]
(Apocynaceae)

The Oleander is a shrub to 4.5 meters with persistent, linear-lanceolate leaves, up to 25 cm in length, that are borne in verticils of three. The plant is aesthetically very pleasing and is resistant to salinity, wind, and parasites. There exist many cultivars having flowers of different colors ranging from darker or lighter pink to white, or with different numbers of petals. *N. oleander* L. is spontaneous in the Mediterranean but is used as an ornamental in all the world's arid climate areas. All parts of the Oleander are extremely poisonous, although certain alkaloids

extracted from the bark are used in treating carcinoma.

ASHANTI BLOOD
Mussaenda erythrophylla Schum. & Thonn. [147]
(Rubiaceae)

This genus counts a goodly number of species that are widely used as ornamentals in gardens in many of the world's tropical countries. The plants are generally shrubs with more or less erect, sometimes climbing, branches. The function of attracting pollinating insects is expedited by the petals and the sepals of the flowers but is greatly aided by the floral bracts, as in *Euphorbia pulcherrima*. *M. erythrophylla*, an African native, has flowers with ovate sepals that are yellow tending to red at the center. There exist many horticultural varieties of this species in which the colors of both the sepals and the bracts may vary.

146

147

Cape Blue Water Lily
Nymphaea capensis
Thunb. 'Pink' 148
(Nymphaeaceae)

Differently from *N. ampla*, which is native to Central America, *N. capensis* Thunb. grows spontaneously in South Africa; it is nevertheless commonly cultivated in many tropical countries. This is a highly variable species, and thanks to this characteristic it has been possible to produce many cultivars with differently-colored flowers and leaves of different dimensions, sometimes variegated.

Passion Flower
Passiflora vitifolia Humb.,
Bonpl. & Klotzl. 149
(Passifloraceae)

The genus *Passiflora* counts more than four hundred species, all native to tropical America. About 50 species have edible fruits; some of these are cultivated commercially and used mainly to produce a juice used for flavoring (Maracuja or Granadilla). The plants are generally vining shrubs with strong tendrils that permit a good anchorage to any type of support, whether woody or rocky. Of the Passion Flowers, the evergreen *P. vitifolia* is that whose leaves most resemble those of the grape (*Vitis*), even though they are smaller, shiny, and thicker. The beautiful blossoms are composed of ten equal and bright red flower parts (five sepals and five petals) around a corona that contains the stamens and the central style.

148

Purple Wreath
Petrea volubilis L. 150
(Verbenaceae)

The general look of *Petra volubilis* L., spontaneous in Central America and the Caribbean, is very much reminiscent of *Congea tomentosa*. The plant is a liana, with branches as long as 15 meters. The opposite, elliptical leaves are rough on the upper surface and have very short petioles. The flowers, of varying intensities of pink, are composed of a tubular portion formed of five dark pink petals that fall after only two or three days, and five petaloid, linear pink sepals that instead persist much longer, assuring the ornamental value of the plant. The flowers are grouped in heavy, elongated, pendulous inflorescences borne on the outside of the crown and so dense that in well-tended individuals they often conceal almost all the underlying leaves. *P. volubilis* 'Albiflora' is a white-flowered cultivar.

149

150▶

152

CAPE LEADWORT
Plumbago auriculata Lam. [152]
(Plumbaginaceae)

Also known as *Plumbago capensis* Thunb., since it is native to South Africa and in particular to Capetown Province. This woody-stemmed scrambling shrub may climb some meters in height if provided with an adequate support.

The alternate, elliptical leaves, up to 5 cm long, are green on the upper surface and light green to whitish underneath. The salver-shaped flowers vary in color from white to blue, with a pronounced vein at the center of each petal. This species is used for hedging, even in shady areas, but requires continual pruning to check its rapid growth.

PINK TRUMPET VINE
Podranea ricasoliana (Tanf.) Sprague [153]
(Bignoniaceae)

This is a climbing shrub native to southern Africa. The persistent, opposite, odd-pinnate leaves are up to 25 cm in length and are composed of nine to thirteen ovate, acute-tipped leaflets, each up to 10 cm long. The flowers are pink with red striations and grouped in subglobose inflorescences.

SHAVING BRUSH TREE
Pseudobombax ellipticum (Humb., Bonpl. & Klotzl.) Dugand. [151] [154]
(Bombacaceae)

Many authors identify this species as *Bombax ellipticum* Humb., Bonpl. & Klotzl., but it has recently been recognized as belonging to the genus *Pseudobombax* of the family Bombacaceae, many members of which have bulging trunks specialized for water storage. The Shaving Brush Tree, native to Central America, is a large plant that is characterized, besides by the distinctive form of its trunk, by its branches, which are opposite and divaricating. The flowers are generally pink or white, enclosed in four bright pink bracts, and borne at the branch tips. At maturity, these bracts bend back like a banana peel to reveal the stamens, which are again pink, up to 15 cm in length, and bunched like a pompom - or the bristles of a shaving brush, as the common name suggests.

153

154

155

FLAME VINE
Pyrostegia ignea
(Vell.) Presl. 155
(Bignoniaceae)

The genus *Pyrostegia* includes various lianas, all with beautiful and variously-colored flowers, that may that may be found climbing on trees, walls, and trellises throughout the Caribbean region. *P. ignea* (or Flame Vine or Orange Trumpet Vine) is native to Brazil. The shiny evergreen leaves are ovate-lanceolate with acute tips and prominent veins. The bright orange flowers are composed of a long tube arching slightly downward, and four lobes, the top lobe being further divided into two parts which

157

at maturity become reflexed. In the Caribbean, *P. ignea* generally flowers between January and April.

TRAVELER'S TREE
Ravenala madagascariensis
Sonn. 156
(Strelitziaceae)

The *arbol del viajero*, or Traveler's Tree or Traveler's Palm, is a giant herb to 16 meters height, native to Madagascar. The name would appear to derive from the fact that travelers could always find cool water trapped inside its huge floral bracts and indeed the very flowers. The stem is simple or branched at the base and, as in all the monocotyledons, is made up of wrapped leaf sheaths. The leaf blade may be as long as 4 meters and is borne at the end of a petiole of equal length. The flowers are very similar to those of other Strelitziaceae (*Strelitzia nicolai* and *S. reginae*), but are smaller, whitish in color, and with a greenish bract.

FIRECRACKER
Russelia equisetiformis Schldl.
& Cham. 157
(Scrophulariaceae)

This is a small shrub just over one meter in height with slender, weeping branches resembling those of the rushes (Juncaceae, hence the old name of *R. juncea* Zucc.), arranged in verticils that recall the form of the Equisetaceae or horsetails, hence the current species epithet *equisetiformis*. The leaves are no more than small, early-falling scales; the plant is thus for all practical purposes aphyllous, and in fact photosynthesis is performed by the green branches. The bright red flowers, tubes 2 to 4 cm in length resembling little firecrackers, are formed of 5 fused petals and are arranged in inflorescences that are particularly attractive to the pollinating hummingbirds.
The Firecracker is native to Mexico, but is commonly used as an ornamental throughout the Caribbean, especially in rock gardens.

156

158

scarcely differentiated the ones from the others and that in nature are distributed above all in central and southern Africa and in western Asia. The stems are underground rhizomes, while all that is seen aboveground is a tuft of rigid, linear, variegated green leaves 40 to 100 cm long. Flowering is a rare event, especially in the horticultural varieties; the inflorescence is nevertheless composed of numerous violet flowers arranged on an elongated axis. The members of this genus tend to revert to the wild state, especially in arid, sun-drenched areas like roadsides and both the sandy and rocky coastal areas.

MOTHER IN LAW'S TONGUE
Sanseviera trifasciata hort. ex Prain. 158
(Agavaceae)

The genus *Sanseviera* counts a great number of species that are only

UMBRELLA TREE
Schefflera actinophylla (Endl.) Harms. 159
(Araliaceae)

The Umbrella Tree is immediately recognizable thanks to the peculiar structure of its digitate foliage. The leaf is made up of 7 to 18 shiny dark green leathery leaflets up to 25 cm long, each borne on a petiole up to 10 cm long. The petioles of the leaflets are joined at the apex of the stalk of the leaf as a whole, giving shape to a sort of umbrella in which the erect handle is formed of the petioles and the 'canopy', which may be as wide as 70 to 80 cm, of the downward-reflexed leaflet blades.

Taken singly, the flowers are small and insignificant, but they are grouped in glomerules of 5 to 10 that resemble blackberries. These are arranged on stalks up to one meter in length that are in turn borne in groups at the apices of the branches, hence another common name of this plant: Octopus Tree.

S. actinophylla, or 'Schefflera with radiating leaves' is native to Australia but is commonly planted as an ornamental in the gardens of the Caribbean area.

159

160

161

SENNA SURATTENSIS (BURM. F.) IRWIN & BARNEBY [160]
(NO COMMON ENGLISH NAME)
(Caesalpiniaceae)

This is a shrub or small tree with a slender trunk and a spreading, globose crown. The leaves are composed of 6 to 10 pairs of oval-to-round leaflets, sometimes with a small apical mucro. The yellow flowers have five petals, of which the upper three are slightly larger than the lower two, and are grouped in dense inflorescences. This species, native to Southeast Asia, is today commonly cultivated, especially for use in roadside plantings, and tends to become naturalized.

CUP OF GOLD
Solandra maxima
(Sesse & Moc.) P. Green [161]
(Solanaceae)

The persistent leaves of this woody climber, native to Mexico, are coriaceous, elliptical to 5 cm and shortly acuminate, on a well-proportioned petiole. The very large flowers are yellowish with a brown-purple vein on the inner side of each of the petals, which are fused into a tube widening into a chalice-like corolla. The Cup of Gold flowers all year round except in high summer.

BIRD-OF-PARADISE
Strelitzia reginae Banks ex Dryand. [162]
(Strelitziaceae)

The species of the genus *Strelitzia*, native to South Africa, are giant herbs to 10 meters height. The stems, like those of the members of the genera *Heliconia* (Heliconiaceae), *Musa* (Musaceae), and *Ravenala* (Strelitziaceae), are herbaceous but quite thick, being composed of the wrapped and united leaf sheaths. The leaf blades are very large, up to 70 cm, and are supported by a petiole up to two meters in length. *S. reginae* (Bird-of-Paradise or Crane Lily), is one of the smallest members of the genus, since the scape is no taller than 1.5 meters and the leaves no longer than 1.7 meters, petiole included. The flowers are orange or yellow, with a deep blue tongue. This is one of the most popular species in the florist trade, both as a potted plant and as a cut flower.

163

BIRD OF PARADISE
Strelitzia nicolai
Reg. & Korm. 163
(Strelitziaceae)

This treelike species differs from
S. reginae above all as regards its
size, as it is the largest species in the
genus. The scape may in fact grow
as tall as 10 meters and the leaves
may be up to 4 meters in length -
more than two of which are
accounted for by the petiole. The
plant flowers almost continuously all
year round with white blossoms
with a blue to purple tongue.

JADE VINE
Strongylodon macrobotrys
A. Gray 164
(Fabaceae)

Native to the Philippines, this is one
of the showiest flowering plants
found in the gardens of the
Caribbean. It is a liana with
branches as long as 30 meters; the
compound leaves have three shiny,
elliptical leaflets, each up to 20 cm
in length and varying in color from
light green to reddish according to
light conditions. The flowers are a
'luminous turquoise' green, 5 to
8 cm long, and grouped more than
100 at a time in rich, pendulous
inflorescences. Both the peduncle of
the inflorescence and the calyxes of
the single flowers are dark purple.
The inflorescence of the Jade Vine is
enormous - and practically repeats
the colors of the leaves, a very rare
occurrence in the plant world.

164

the ends of the branches, which tend to bend under their weight. The species is native to Capetown Province (South Africa), and is used to good advantage as a decorative touch in tropical gardens, since its brilliantly-colored flowers contrast pleasingly with the dark green of the crown.

BE-STILL TREE
Thevetia peruviana (Pers.) K. Schum. |167|
(Apocynaceae)

This small shrub, 4 to 8 meters in height, is native to the tropical-climate areas of the Americas. It is widespread in the Caribbean, where it is used as an ornamental mainly along roadsides and generally in dry locations. The leaves are linear, shiny on the upper surface, and much reminiscent of those of the Oleander (*Nerium oleander* L.); for this reason the Be-Still Tree is also classified as *T. neriifolia* Juss. and also known commonly as Yellow Oleander. The bright yellow flowers are composed of a tubular portion about 3 cm in length and a portion that expands gradually to form 5 wide-based lobes. All parts of this plant, as is the case in the overwhelming majority of the species of the family Apocynaceae, are extremely poisonous due to the whitish latex they contain. The latex of this particular species is rich in a natural alkaloid that produces effects very similar to those of digitalis, and like digitalis is used in compounding cardiac stimulants.

165

167

TAMARIND
Tamarindus indica L. |165|
(Caesalpiniaceae)

T. indica, the sole species in the genus *Tamarindus*, is native to tropical Africa, whence it has been introduced into most of the rest of the world's tropical-climate areas. The genus name derives from the Arabic *tamr hindi* = Indian date; the species epithet only stresses the relation with India. The Tamarind is a tree growing to considerable size: up to 30 meters in height with a trunk to 4 meters in diameter. The trunk is tall and graceful and the dense, rounded crown is often borne high up on a long length of nude trunk. The leaves are bipinnate and the flowers are small, yellow in color, and grouped in rounded inflorescences. The fruits, which have made a name for this tree worldwide, are cylindrical legumes up to 30 cm in length, subdivided by constrictions between the seeds, green when young and dark brown when ripe. This plant has been used in medicine since the 11th century BC, as a laxative and to combat scurvy, and also in treatment of liver disorders and intoxications. The leaves are used to prepare infusions for treating diarrhea, dysentery, diabetes, and eye irritations. The edible fruit is widely cultivated in India, where it is used in the preparation of many foods and drinks. The Tamarind was introduced to the Caribbean region in the early 19th century.

166

CAPE HONEYSUCKLE
Tecomaria capensis (Thunb.) Spach 'Lutea' |166|
(Bignoniaceae)

This shrub, sometimes with pendent branches, grows to 2 meters height. The leaves are opposite and shiny dark green in color. The flowers are red, brilliant orange, or yellow as in the 'Lutea' garden variety. The five petals are fused to form a slightly curving tube up to 7 cm long that opens into short lobes with the stamens projecting beyond the corolla. The flowers are grouped in dense inflorescences near

Bengal Clock Vine
Thunbergia grandiflora (Roxb. ex Rottl.) Roxb. 168
(Acanthaceae)

The genus Thunbergia counts a great number of species, most of which native to Southeast Asia, that are often cultivated as ornamental plants for use in hedges and are naturalized almost everywhere, above all along the roads. *T. grandiflora*, like many of the species present in Central America, is a liana whose branches may grow as long as 20 meters. The opposite leaves are lanceolate to heart-shaped, with rough surfaces. The flowers, which appear singly or in groups of 2 to 4, vary in color from purplish-pink to blue with cream-white centers. Up to 8 cm wide, they consist of a tubular portion and a spreading, campanulate portion with five slightly unequal lobes, the lower center lobe being a little larger than the others. Other species of *Thunbergia* cultivated in the Caribbean islands include *T. laurifolia* Lindl., from the Malay peninsula, with thick leaves and sky-blue flowers in groups of 6 to 10; *T. alata* Boj. ex Sims, or Black-Eyed-Susan Vine, native to East Africa, with yellow or orange flowers and of considerable importance as a food source for hummingbirds; *T. fragrans* Roxb., from Southeast Asia, with its whitish flowers no more than 3 cm across.

168

Spider Lily
Tradescantia pallida (Rose) D. Hunt 169
(Commelinaceae)

T. pallida (Rose) D. Hunt, sometimes indicated as *Setcresea purpurea* Boom., is a creeping herb with lanceolate-linear leaves up to 25 cm long, with parallel veins and metallic purple in color. The three-petaled, light pink flowers are tiny. This species grows spontaneously in Mexico and Texas, but it is widely used in flowerbeds in many tropical areas to create perennial touches of color. The plant tends to become spontaneous in dry, sunny areas, and can well tolerate a certain degree of salinity.

169

Glossary

Acuminate. Tapering to a slender point.

Acute. Abruptly pointed.

Alkaloid. An organic base containing nitrogen, of various chemical composition. Many alkaloids are poisonous and active, above all on the nervous system, even at very small doses.

Annual. A plant that completes its life-cycle (germination from seed, flowering, fruiting, death) in a single season.

Anther. The terminal portion of the stamen in which the pollen is produced.

Anthropization. The actions of man that aim at transforming and modifying of the territory to adapt it to serve his interests and needs.

Aphyllous. Without leaves.

Aristate. Having a slender, sharp, spine-like tip.

Awn. A small, pointed process or bristle.

Axil. The angle between the leaf and the stem.

Axis. Flower- or leaf-bearing stem (primary axis) or branch or peduncle (secondary axis).

Bipinnate. Of a leaf divided into segments, each of which is again divided into segments.

Blade. The broad portion of a leaf.

Bract. A modified and usually small leaf (often scale-like, sometimes leaf-like) located near a flower or an inflorescence.

Bulb. The ovoid underground part of certain plants (mostly monocotyledonous herbs) composed of a mass of overlapping fleshy or membranous leaves on a short stem base.

Caducous. Falling off easily or before the usual time.

Calyx. The outer whorl of a flower, composed of the sepals which envelop the flower and protect it in the bud.

Campanulate. Bell-shaped.

Cauline. Belonging to or growing on a stem; specifically, growing on the upper portion of a stem.

Caulis. Stem or stalk.

Compound. Of an organ, generally a leaf, formed of several elements.

Corolla. Collective name for the petals that form the involucre of a flower.

Culm. A hollow or pithy herbaceous stem.

Cultivar. A cultivated variety obtained from a spontaneous plant through complex processes of selection and hybridization. The term was introduced to botanical language in 1952, when during the 13th Horticultural Congress it was decided to apply it to cultivated varieties of plants to distinguish them from natural varieties.

Cuneate. Wedge-shaped; narrowly triangular with an acute angle toward the base.

Cyanogenetic. Capable of producing cyanide.

Cyathium. A type of inflorescence peculiar to the Spurges (*Euphorbiaceae*) consisting of a cup-like involucre surrounding several male flowers and one female flower or only the male flowers or a single female flower.

Cyme. An inflorescence terminating in an apical flower.

Deciduous. Having non-persistent leaves, flowers, etc., which fall at the end of the their functional period. Having or made up of deciduous parts (as a deciduous tree).

Dentate. Having acute, outward-pointing projections (as a leaf margin).

Digitate. With finger-like lobes; generally used of a leaf or bract.

Distal. Remote from the point of attachment or origin.

Dorsiventral. Extending from back to front (dorsal to ventral side).

Ecology. The science of the interrelationships among living organisms and the environment in which they live. The term was coined in 1869 by the German biologist E. Haeckel.

Ecosystem. The set of living organisms and non-biological constituents (sub-strate, climate, solar radiation, etc.) that interact in a given area.

Elliptical. Thinner at the base and the apex with the broadest portion near the center.

Endemic. Exclusive to a given area; may refer to species, genus, or even family.

Entire. Not toothed; of margins of leaves or petals.

Epiphyte. A plant that grows upon another plant non-parasitically or on an object and derives its water and nutrients from the air and rain and sometimes the debris accumulating around it. Also called 'air plant'.

Family. In zoological and botanical classification, a group of related plants or animals forming a category ranking above a genus and below an order.

Filiform. Having the shape of a thread or filament.

Flora. The plants characteristic of, peculiar to, or adapted to living in a particular situation (geographical area, country, etc.).

Form. A botanical taxonomic category ranking below a variety and differing from related forms in only a few characters.

Formation. A unit of study of vegetation, comprising the aggregate of the forms of the individuals that share similar ecological conditions.

Genus. A taxonomic category ranking between the family and the species, comprising a group of structurally or phylogenetically related species or an isolated species exhibiting unusual differentiation.

Glabrous. Having a smooth even surface devoid of hairs or down.

Gland. An organ secreting salt, water, sugar solutions, or other substances.

Glaucous. Having a powdery or waxy coating that gives a frosted appearance.

Globose. Globe-like, rounded.

Glomerule. A globular inflorescence composed of numerous flowers clustered together.

Gramineous. Resembling or relating to a grass.

Habitat. The set of climatic and environmental conditions that permit single animal or plant species to live and develop; the kind of site or region naturally or normally preferred by a biological species.

Herb. Any green-stemmed plant that does not develop a woody stem.

Herbaceous. Of plant organs that are green and with a leaf-like texture.

Hybrid. A plant originating from cross-breeding between two distinct species.

Inflorescence. A floral axis with its appendages; a flower cluster or sometimes a solitary flower.

Infructescence. The fruiting stage of an inflorescence.

Involucre. Flower-bracts forming a cuff or ruff at the base of a flower cluster or flowerhead.

Lanceolate. Shaped like a lance head, wider at the base and tapering to a point at the apex.

Leaflet. One of the divisions of a compound leaf.

Legume. A dehiscent fruit formed of a single carpel, typical of the family *Leguminosae*, which at maturity opens along the two sides to release the seeds.

Lianas. Woody perennial vines with rope-like stems that climb to the crowns of trees. Leafing, flowering, and fruiting generally takes place only at growth tips.

Lignify. To become woody, used of stems or branches.

Lithophyte. A plant that has adapted to living on a rocky substrate.

Lobed. Divided, but not separated entirely, into various parts by deeper or shallower notches.

Locule. Cavity in a fruit.

Monocotyledon. A plant having a single cotyledon (the first leaf developed by a germinating plant; also called seed leaf).

Mucro. Abrupt sharp terminal point or process of a plant part.

Mycorrhiza. The symbiotic association of a fungus with the roots of a seed plant.

Naturalized species. A species adapted to growing and reproducing naturally in areas outside its native distribution area.

Oblanceolate. Inversely lanceolate.

Oblong. Longer than wide, with parallel sides for the greater part of the length.

Obovate. Inversely ovate: ovate with the narrower end basal.

Obtuse. Of a leaf: blunt or rounded at the end.

Orbiculate. Circular or nearly circular in shape.

Ovate. Egg-shaped, with the basal end broader.

Palmate. Hand-like, with generally shallow lobes, venation, or segments all radiating from a common point.

Pedicel. The stalk of an individual flower.

Peduncle. Generally, the supporting stalk of a leaf, flower, etc.

Pendent. Supported from above; hanging.

Perennial. A plant living for a number of years, and often long-lived.

Perianth. The external sterile parts of a flower (calyx and corolla).

Persistent. Enduring beyond the normal time, as opposed to caducous and deciduous.

Petal. One of the members comprising the corolla of a flower.

Petaloid. Brightly colored and resembling a petal.

Petiole. The leaf-stalk.

Photosynthesis. The process of transformation of the light energy absorbed by the pigments of plant cells containing chlorophyll into chemical energy, by which inorganic substances (carbon dioxide, water) are transformed into organic substances (carbohydrates). The photosynthetic process releases oxygen, a requisite for animal life.

Pinnate. Having similar parts arranged on opposite sides of an axis, like a feather; used especially of compound leaves, in which the number of leaflets may be even or odd. See also **Bipinnate**.

Pioneer. A species capable of colonizing a bare or barren area and initiating a new ecological cycle.

Propagulum. A propagable shoot.

Pseudobulb. A solid bulbous enlargement of a stem.

Puberulent. Minutely downy; covered with a fine pubescence.

Pubescent. Covered with fine, soft, short hairs.

Recurved. Turned backwards in a curve.

Reflexed. Bent or curved backward or downward.

Relict. A persistent remnant of an otherwise (locally or generally) extinct flora or vanishing type.

Reticulate. Having veins, fibers, or lines crossing like the threads or fibers of a network.

Retuse. Rounded or obtuse with a slight notch.

Rhizome. A modified stem that grows horizontally underground; often serves as a deposit for reserve food material.

Root. A portion of the plant body of a seed plant, lacking nodes, buds and leaves; usually underground, it is used by the plant as an organ of anchorage and for absorbing water and nutritive substances.

Rosette. A cluster of leaves, often overlapping, growing out in all directions around a single center point. May be either basal or apical.

Ruderal. Of a species or vegetation growing in an environment greatly modified by man.

Scandent. Climbing.

Scape. Often leafless, flower-bearing axis.

Scorpioid. Having a concentric arrangement of parts.

Scrambler. A plant that spreads over other vegetation or its substrate.

Scrub. Of a stunted tree or shrub growing to maximum 5 meters with a single, but non-dominant, stem, giving the appearance of equal height and breadth; a vegetation formation dominated by such individuals.

Sepal. A single element of the calyx of a flower.

Sessile. Unstalked; of an organ (flower, leaf, fruit, etc.) joined directly to its support, with no peduncle.

Sheath. The lower part of the leaf surrounding the stem.

Shrub. A several-stemmed woody plant, in which no one axis dominates over the others.

Spathe. A bract of variable color and size, subtending an inflorescence.

Spatulate. Spatula-shaped, narrow at the base and widest toward the apex.

Species. Basic unit of zoological and botanical classification ranking immediately below a genus or subgenus, comprised of interbreeding organisms that ordinarily comprise differentiated populations.

Spiciform. Spike-shaped.

Spike. An inflorescence formed of an axis bearing, laterally, sessile or subsessile flowers.

Spine. A stiff, sharply-pointed organ derived from modification of a leaf, stipule, root, stem or branch.

Stalk. Axis, stem.

Stamen. One of the male elements of the reproductive apparatus of a flower, consisting of a stalk or filament supporting the anther.

Station. An area of variable size that is uniform from the point of view of the ecological parameters referred to the physical environment.

Stem. A generally aerial plant part that supports secondary branches, leaves, etc.

Stipule. A leaf- or scale-like structure of varying form and size located at the base of the leaf.

Stolon. Creeping stem (horizontal branch) that produces new plants from buds at its tip or nodes. Also called runner.

Style. The stalk that connects the stigma to the ovary.

Subglobose. Nearly globose.

Subspecies. Unit of classification ranking immediately below a species, designated on the basis of constant discriminating characters but also separated geographically or ecologically.

Succulent. Having fleshy tissues containing water.

Symbiontic. Of an organism living in symbiosis, usually referred to the smaller member of a symbiotic pair.

Symbiosis. The living together of two dissimilar organisms in mutually beneficial relationships.

Subsaline. Salty but not excessively so.

Tepal. Any of the modified leaves making up the perianth of a flower when petals (generally colored) and sepals (generally green) are not distinguishable in the corolla.

Terrigenous. Formed by the erosive action of rivers, tides, and currents.

Thermophyte. A plant that requires or thrives best at elevated temperatures.

Thermoxerophyte. A plant adapted for life and growth at elevated temperatures and with a limited water supply.

Tomentose. Covered with cottony downy hairs.

Tomentum. Pubescence composed of matted wooly hairs.

Tree. A woody perennial plant, generally large in size, having one erect main axis or stem dominating the others; generally taller than it is wide.

Tube. An often cylindrical, fused part of a corolla or calyx.

Umbel. An inflorescence in which the flowers are all at the same level and the flower stalks all arise from the same point, like the spokes of an umbrella.

Undulate. Wavy; of leaf or petal margins.

Unisexual. Of a flower with only stamens or only a pistil.

Variety. A subdivision of a species or subspecies and differing from related varieties in only a few a often even only one character.

Vegetation. Group of individuals belonging to one or more species that share the water, light, and nutritive resources of a given space at a given time.

Vegetative. Of or relating to propagation by nonsexual processes or methods.

Verticil. A circle or whorl of similar parts (as flowers or leaves) about a point on an axis.

Vimineous. Of or producing slender twigs or shoots.

Vine. Loose assemblage of plants that undergo the process of vining, or elongation of the stem, and tend to climb vertically but lack the ability to sustain their weight without support. Types include lianas, climbers, and scramblers.

Viviparous. In botany, germinating while still attached to the parent plant.

Weeping. Having slender, pendent branches.

Index of Scientific Names

Index of Common English Names

Bibliography

Adams C. D. 1972. *Flowering Plants of Jamaica.* University of the West Indies, Mona, Jamaica.

Alain H. L. 1981. *Flora of Hispaniola. Part 1.* New Jersey.

Alain H. L. 1983-1985. *Flora de la Espanola. II-III.* San Pedro de Macoris.

Alain H. L. & L. F. Martorell. 1982. *Flora of Puerto Rico and Adjacent Islands: A Systematic Synopsis.* University of Puerto Rico, Corripio, Santo Domingo.

Beard R. W. 1980. Notes on Palmae. *I. Phytologia* 46(5): 285-287.

Beccari O. 1908. Le palme americane della Tribù delle Corypheae. *Webbia* 2: 1-343.

Borhidi A. 1991. *Phytogeography and Vegetation Ecology of Cuba.* Akademiai Kiado, Budapest.

Bourne M. J., G.W. Lennox & S. A. Seddon. 1988. *Fruits and Vegetables of the Caribbean.* Mac Millan Caribbean, London.

Bramwell D. 1979. *Plants and Islands.* Academic Press, London.

Carrington S. 1993. *Wild Plants of Barbados.* Mac Millan Education, London.

Carrington S. 1998. *Wild Plants of the Eastern Caribbean.* Mac Millan Education, London.

Coleridge H. N. 1825. *Six Months in the West Indies.* London.

Collett J. & P. Bowe. 1998. *Gardens of the Caribbean.* Mac Millan Education, London.

Correll D. S. & H. B. Correll. 1982. *Flora of the Bahama Archipelago.* J. Cramer, Vaduz.

Hargreaves D. & B. Hargreaves. 1960. *Tropical Blossoms of the Caribbean.* Ross-Hargreaves, Hawaii.

Honychurch P. N. 1986. *Caribbean Wild Plants and Their Uses.* Mac Millan Caribbean, London.

Howard A. R. 1979. Flora of West Indies. In Larsen K., *Tropical Botany.* Academic Press, London.

Kingsbury J. M. 1988. *200 Conspicuous, Unusual, or Economically Important Tropical Plants of the Caribbean.* Bullbrier Press, Ithaca, NY.

Lack J. A., C. Whitefoord, P. G. H. Evans, J. Arlington & H. Greenop. 1997. *Illustrated Flora. Dominica Nature Island of the Caribbean.* Ministry of Tourism, Commonwealth of Dominica.

Lennox G. W. & S. A. Seddon. 1978. *Flowers of the Caribbean.* Mac Millan Caribbean, London.

Little E. L. Jr., R O. Woodbury & F. H. Wadsworth. 1974. *Trees of Puerto Rico and the Virgin Islands.* Agriculture Handbook No. 449, U.S. Department of Agriculture, Washington.

Loveless A. R. 1960. The Vegetation of Antigua, West Indies. *J. Ecol.* 48: 495-527.

Mac Gillavry H. J. 1970. Geological History of the Caribbean. *Konikl. Nedersl. Akad. Weternsch. Proc. Ser. B* 73: 289-295.

Magras M. 1989. *Caribbean Flowers.* Latanier ed., S. Barthelemy.

Muniz O. & A. Borhidi. 1982. Catalogo de las palmas de Cuba. *Acta Bot. Acad. Scie. Hung.* 28: 309-345.

Nellis D. W. 1994. *Seashore Plants of South Florida and the Caribbean.* Pineapple Press, Sarasota, Florida.

Schaw J. 1939. *Journal of a Lady of Quality.* Third edition, Yale University Press, New Haven.

Seddon S. A. & G. W. Lennox. 1980. *Trees of the Caribbean.* Mac Millan Caribbean, London.

Trollope A. 1859. *The West Indies and the Spanish Main.* London.

Warren W. 1997. *Tropical Plants for Home and Garden.* Thames and Hudson Ltd, London.

Williams R. O. 1969. *The Useful and Ornamental Plants of Trinidad and Tobago.* Government Press, Trinidad.

Wyse Jackson P. & J. Willison. 1996. *Plant Conservation in the Caribbean Islands – the Role of Botanic Gardens.* Botanic Garden Conservation International, Richmond.